AF572610

STAR
VOYAGE

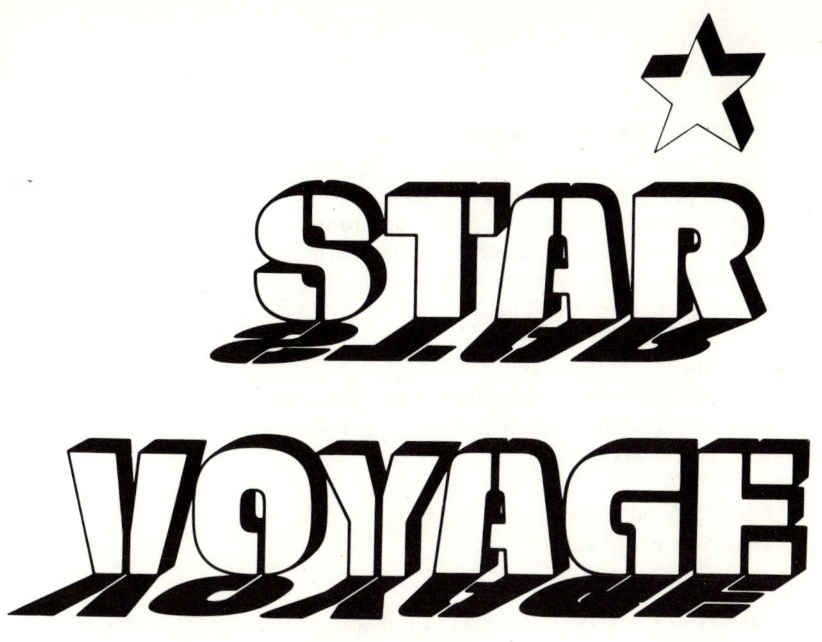

by Joseph J. DiCerto

Illustrated with diagrams by the author and photographs

Julian Messner

New York

Published by Julian Messner, a Simon & Schuster
Division of Gulf & Western Corporation,
Simon & Schuster Building,
1230 Avenue of the Americas,
New York, New York 10020.
JULIAN MESSNER and colophon are trademarks of
Simon & Schuster, registered in the U.S. Patent
And Trademark Office.

Manufactured in the United States of America.
Design by Philip Jaget

Library of Congress Cataloging in Publication Data

DiCerto, J. J.
Star voyage.

Includes index.
Summary: Describes the problems of travel in space,
life on a space station and in a space colony, and
possibilities and theories regarding extraterrestrial
life.
1. Interplanetary voyages—Juvenile literature.
2. Space colonies—Juvenile literature. [1. Interplanetary voyages. 2. Space colonies] I. Title.
TL793.D49 629.4 81-808
ISBN 0-671-33034-9 AACR2

TO MY PRECIOUS SON DAVID, WHOSE ASPIRATIONS AND DREAMS ARE AS BROAD AND ENDLESS AS THE COSMOS.

A BIG THANKS TO LESTER GAVER OF NASA
FOR HIS CHEERFUL AND VALUABLE HELP.

Messner books by **Joseph J. DiCerto**
STAR VOYAGE
FROM EARTH TO INFINITY
A Guide to Space Travel

CONTENTS

Chapter 1

Space Unlimited

We are about to start on a journey which will take us through the vast, mysterious, uncharted reaches of space, something that human beings have dreamed about for thousands of years.

We are going to take a star voyage.

Once we leave, there will be no turning back. We will spend the rest of our lives as space travelers, forever journeying through the Universe.

"Universe" is a word we use to describe everything that exists. The universe contains the Earth, everything on the Earth, all the space around the Earth. It is the sun, all the planets, all the stars, and the clouds of dust and gas between the stars. All the life on Earth or on other distant worlds is part of the universe. Scientists refer to the universe as "the totality of existence."

We know that the universe is unbelievably vast, but the exact size will always remain a mystery. In order to get some idea of the huge size of the universe, compare other distances. The Earth is 25,000 miles around at the equator, the widest part of the globe of Earth. It would take a rocket flying at 1,000 miles per hour 25 hours to fly around the world at this point.

Earth's nearest neighbor, the moon, is 240,000 miles away. It would take the same rocket flying at the same speed 240 hours to reach the moon.

The sun is a lot farther away: 93 million miles. To make this trip, our rocket would have to travel for 93,000 hours—over ten years.

The nearest star beyond the sun, Alpha Centauri, is 26 trillion miles from earth, almost 300 times farther away than the sun—a flight of 3,000 years for our rocket. Other stars are a million times farther. Yet even these stars are not at the end of the Universe. There may be stars so far away that we cannot see them even with powerful telescopes.

Some scientists think that there may be no end to the universe. So they say that the size of the universe is "infinite," without end.

Hercules Star Cluster.

Once we are on our journey to a star you will soon realize that the stars are not scattered throughout the universe separately. You will see groups or clusters of stars, fairly evenly distributed. These clusters are called "galaxies." Scientists estimate that there are about 100 billion galaxies in the universe. And the average galaxy may contain about 100 billion stars.

Galaxies come in many sizes—all of them big—and also in different shapes. Some are in the shape of a giant sphere, or ball. Some are flattened and are known as "disc galaxies." Millions of years of rotating may develop disc galaxies into "spiral galaxies," with trailing arms. Spiral galaxies are shaped like pinwheels. Our own Milky Way is a spiral galaxy. Our sun is located in one of the trailing arms of the galaxy about 25,000 to 30,000 light-years from the center.

The center of a galaxy is usually crammed with hundreds of billions of stars. The centers of galaxies may also be the location of mysterious astronomical bodies such as pulsars, quasars, and black holes, which will be described later.

The stars in a galaxy vary in size and age. Some stars burn for billions of years, after which they become dwarf stars: cold, black cinders in space. More massive stars live for only a few million years, then they explode. For a short while these stars, called "supernovas," give off an amount of light equivalent to billions of stars.

When they run out of fuel and die, supernovas may collapse and compact together into small objects called "neutron stars," only 10 miles or so in diameter. A neutron star is so dense, so compacted, that a spoonful of its material would weigh thousands of tons. Neutron stars have extremely powerful gravity. If you could stand on the surface of one, you would weigh hundreds of millions of tons.

Neutron stars act as very powerful magnets. This led astronomers to discover another type of star. In 1968 a young college student, Jocelyn Bell, noticed strange signals on an electronic instrument connected to his telescope. The signals kept repeating, like the ticking of a clock, and were coming from far out in space. At first scientists thought they might be signals from a distant civilization. But after some investigation, they realized that the signals were coming from a mysterious stellar body, which they named a "pulsar," for pulsating star.

A pulsar, as it turns out, is a rapidly rotating neutron star. Like a space lighthouse, its powerful magnetic force generates a beam of energy sweeping through space. Earth receives a pulse of energy each time the force field of the neutron star sweeps by us. Some neutron stars rotate as fast as 1,000 revolutions per second. Scientists now think that there may be as many as 100,000 pulsars in our galaxy, the Milky Way.

In the early 1960s, scientists using a special type of electronic telescope known as a "radio telescope" located a stellar object that was producing an enormous amount of energy. All stars produce various types of energy or radiation, radio waves being one of them. But whatever this object was, it was generating as much radio energy as hundreds of billions of stars, and it was extremely far away. In fact, the signals had left the object about 3 *billion* years before. For a while, scientists could not believe their instruments. But then they found similar objects in other locations. They named these cosmic bodies "quasars," which stands for quasi-stellar (starlike) radio sources. Just recently a

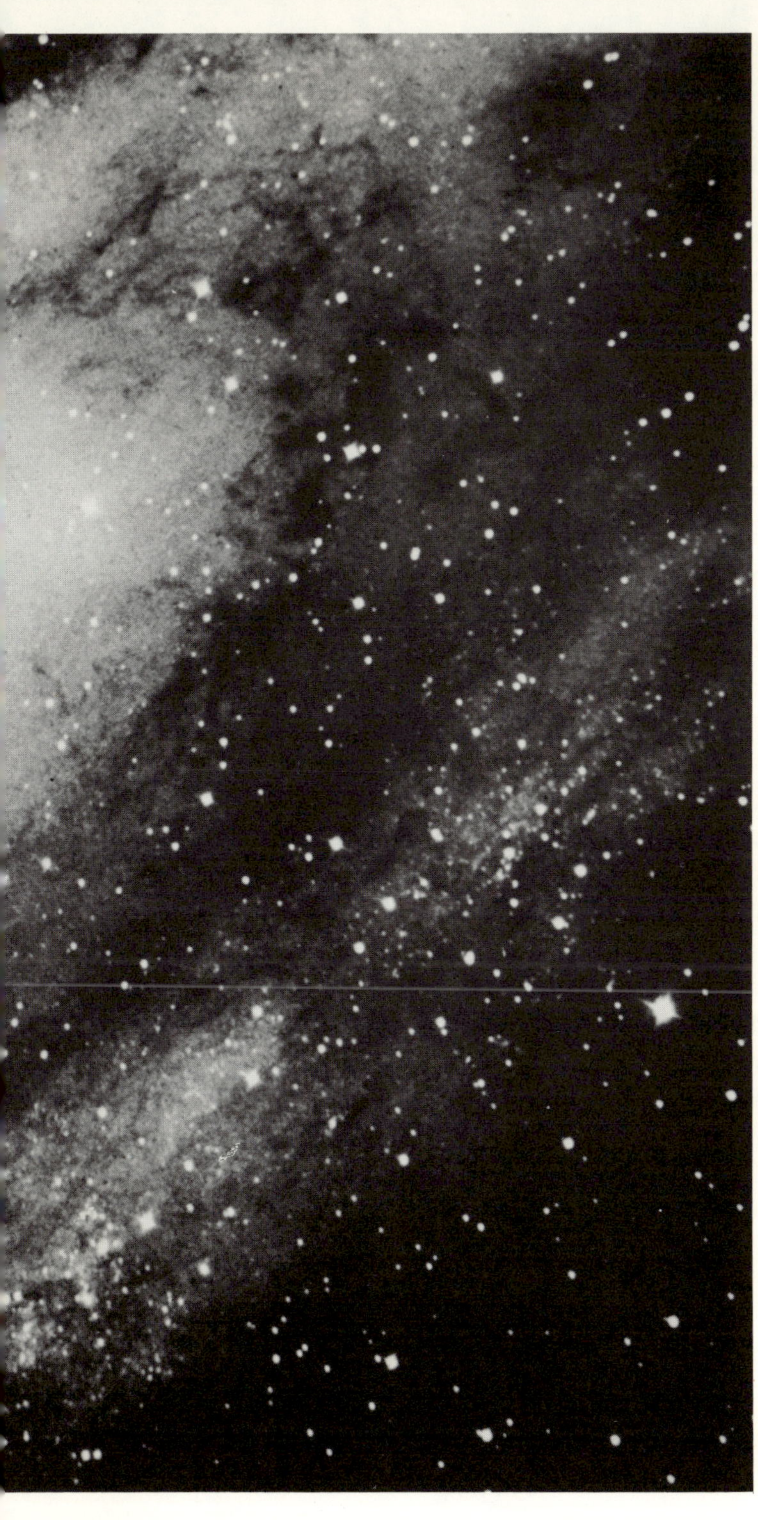

Great Galaxy
in Andromeda.

quasar was located at a distance of 15 billion light-years from us. Scientists believe that the signals that we are just now receiving from this distant object started racing toward us billions of years before our solar system was even formed!

In 1967, another stellar object was discovered. Like the quasar, it gave off a tremendous amount of energy. But the energy from this body was in the form of visible light rather than radio waves. This object was given the name "BL Lacertae," or "BL Lac" for short. BL Lacs are powerhouses of energy. They shine with the light of 10 billion suns and are the brightest objects in the universe. In 1975, one such BL Lac flared up and became as bright as one thousand trillion stars. Scientists cannot explain how any object can possibly produce that much light.

Now, picture the following scene. A large spacecraft is speeding through space. It has a crew of 500, a starship with large control rooms, engine rooms, dining rooms, and bedrooms. Obviously, it is a huge structure. Suddenly, before your very eyes, in an instant, it disappears. Science fiction? Not necessarily. The spacecraft might have stumbled upon a "black hole." What strange sort of space monster is this black hole that it can cause a giant spacecraft to disappear?

To understand a black hole, one must return to the death of stars. We have seen that some stars simply dim and collapse into dwarf stars, while large stars collapse into super-dense neutron stars. But if a star is *very* large, say 30 times more massive than our sun, and it collapses, a totally different type of body is formed.

The mass of this giant star collapses with a tremendous force. This force is so great that the matter of the star is compressed, crushed, into an object thousands of times smaller than it was. A star, which may have had a diameter of 5 million miles can be compressed into a tiny sphere which may measure only 50 feet or less—a black hole. So compressed or dense is the material of a black hole that a teaspoon of it would weigh billions or even trillions of tons. This incredible density has a gravity pull that is the strongest force in the universe—nothing can overcome its power. As a result of this terrible gravity, anything that comes near a black hole is instantly sucked in. Not only is it sucked in, but it is crushed down to a microscopic speck.

That is what happened to our imaginary spacecraft. But why couldn't the spacecraft crew see the black hole and steer around it? Because a black hole is invisible.

That's right, invisible. We see objects because light bounces off their surfaces and carries the image into our eyes. But if you were to stand in a pitch-dark room, you would not be able to see any of the objects in the room. There might be chairs, tables, lamps, pictures on the walls, but all these things would be invisible.

This is also true of black holes, those ultra-strange cosmic ghosts. Light cannot escape from its powerful gravity—and without light escaping or bouncing off its surface, a black hole is invisible.

Suppose we could watch that spacecraft approaching the black hole. First it enters into what is called the "accretion disc." Accretion means "to gather." The craft—any matter—is caught in the accretion disc as though it were caught in the outer fringe of a whirlpool. The craft begins to spiral downward toward the black hole. The farther into the "whirlpool" matter goes, the harder it is to escape, until, after a while, the spacecraft reaches the "event horizon." This is the point of no return. Now the spacecraft is under the control of the black hole's enormous pull of gravity. The spacecraft is torn apart and crushed into the heart of the black hole. (This area has been given the mysterious name of "singularity.") All the matter of the spacecraft has now been crushed into nothingness.

Scientists believe that black holes may be the energy source behind quasars and BL Lacs. It is believed that black holes the size of 1 billion suns provide the power for quasars.

Some scientists think that black holes exist in the centers of galaxies and large star clusters. They suspect that in the center of one giant galaxy (M87), there may be a black hole as massive as 5 billion suns. They believe they have located a black hole in the constellation Cygnus X-1. There they have located what seems to be a double, or binary, star. However, they can see only one star. They can tell by the movement of that star that a second star exists. Single stars move in a special path, known to scientists. When a star is not moving as it should, something or some force is affecting it, causing it to wobble. Scientists think that this odd motion is being caused by the gravity of another star that is close by but cannot be seen. They believe that the second star is a black hole and that the black hole is actually consuming its companion star.

Astronomers calculate that there may be as many as 1 billion black holes in our galaxy alone. Are black holes sucking up the universe? Where does all the matter go when it enters a black hole? Does a black hole merely continue to compress countless trillions of tons of matter into its innards? Maybe not. Some

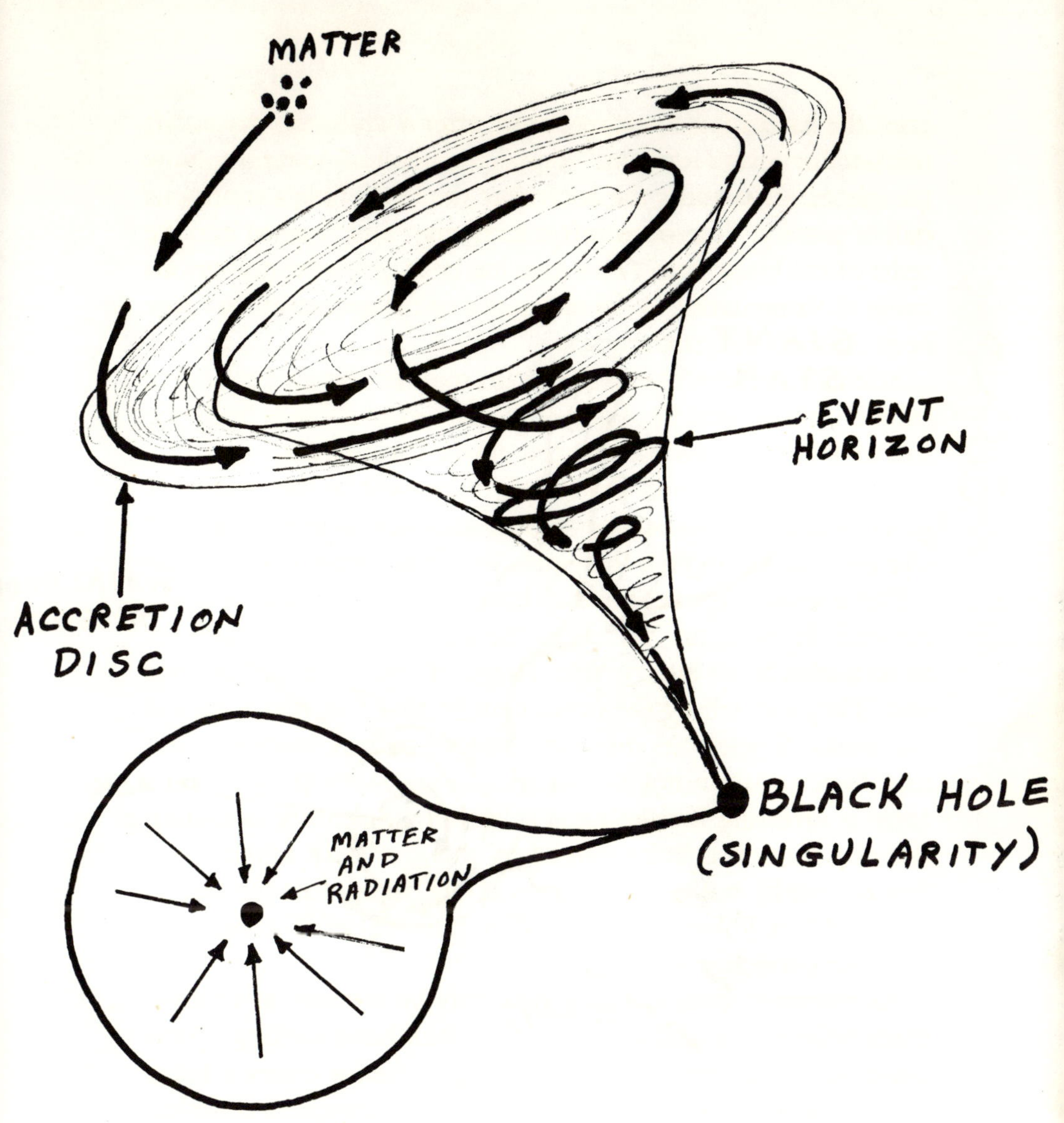

Not even light can escape from the powerful gravitational hold of a black hole.

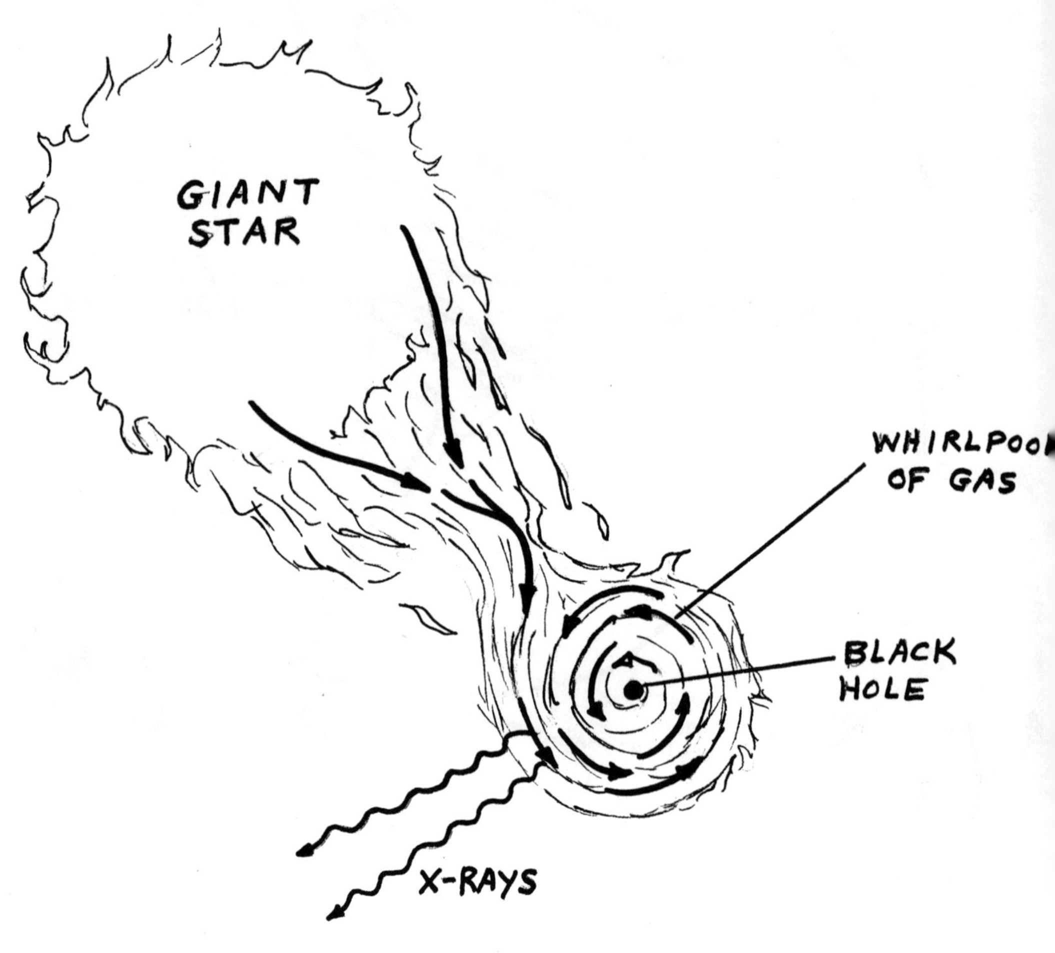

A black hole at Cygnus X-1 may be consuming its neighboring star.

scientists think that a black hole may be a mysterious passageway to another part of the universe. In other words, matter that is sucked into a black hole might instantly reappear somewhere else. The point from which it emerges is called, naturally, a "white hole."

Surely there is nothing stranger in the pages of science fiction than can be found in our universe.

However, even if we were to travel at nearly the speed of light, it would be many years before we would have to worry about encountering such fearsome objects as black holes. What we must concern ourselves with now are the machines that will carry us through space and all the equipment we will need to stay alive after we leave the protective arms of Earth.

Chapter 2

The First Step of a Long Journey

There is really nothing natural about our living in space. Once we venture into the black vacuum, free of Earth's demanding gravity, we must become adapted to a totally new environment. Every aspect of living—eating, sleeping, working, playing, bathing—takes on a different nature. Just keeping a human being alive in space is no easy task.

A human being can remain alive only within a narrow set of limits. Consider atmospheric pressure, for example. Humans have developed in an atmosphere of 14.7 pounds per square inch. We know if a person moves too far from this general pressure range, death is certain.

Temperature is another limiting factor on human life. The human body must be maintained fairly close to 98.6° F.

Another basic requirement for life is oxygen. Three minutes without oxygen can result in severe brain damage. Five minutes without oxygen can mean death.

Then there's water—without it a person would expire in about a week.

Finally, there's food, the fuel that keeps the machinery of our bodies in operation.

All these life necessities are taken for granted on Earth. In space they are nonexistent. So when you venture into space, you must take your environment along.

This is accomplished through the use of a lot of machines and complex electronic equipment, a *life support system.*

A life support system keeps the air clean. In a modern space station, air is pumped through filters which clean and purify it. Dust, food crumbs, and so on are removed by a first set of filters. Then the air is forced through a second set of filters which contain charcoal, a substance that removes unwanted body and food odors and certain gases. But the air is still not ready to be sent back to the cabin, because it may contain small amounts, called "trace quantities," of poisonous gases. So after leaving the charcoal filters, the air enters a machine called a "catalytic burner." In this unit all traces of poisonous gases are removed. From here, the air flows through "heat exchangers," to bring the air to the proper temperature for cabin use.

One of the reasons that life support systems work successfully is that they can recycle air and water. Air and water are not really destroyed when we use them. For example, when you inhale and take oxygen into your body, the oxygen is not lost. When the oxygen has performed its duties, you exhale it as carbon dioxide (CO_2). When the oxygen is separated from the carbon dioxide, it can be used over and over again. So the oxygen present in a small room would sustain you for a lifetime, if it were recycled by a life support system.

The "oxygen recovery system" is the part of the life support system that recycles oxygen. A CO_2 concentrator captures all the CO_2 out of the air. Then a second part of the oxygen recovery system separates the captured CO_2 into carbon (C) and oxygen (O_2), after which the oxygen is returned for use in the cabin air supply. Additional supplies of oxygen are kept on board to make up for any loss of oxygen through airlock doors, etcetera.

Without water, we could not survive on Earth or in space. And there are no water holes in space. So the life support system has to ensure that we have a reasonable supply of water.

Water is taken into our bodies a number of ways: in its pure form; in beverages such as soda, milk, coffee, and tea; and in the food we eat. The water also leaves our bodies in different ways. We eliminate it as water vapor in breathing, as perspiration, as urine, or as solid waste (feces).

Perspiration evaporates along with the moisture in our breath and becomes suspended in the cabin atmosphere, increasing the humidity level. This moisture, which is part oxygen, is removed by the air recycling part of the life support system.

Urine is also recycled to obtain pure water. Urine and waste water from washing are collected in a storage tank until there is enough to begin the recycling process. Special chemicals are added to the tank to prevent bacteria from growing and also to prevent the formation of harmful gases. Then the liquids are passed through a special machine which removes all the solid particles. This is done by boiling the water and forcing the steam which is produced through charcoal filters. These filters also remove any odors from the steam. Next, the steam is cooled back to water, and the water is returned to the spacecraft water supply.

On your space journey it will be common for individuals and groups to venture out into the vacuum—airlessness—of space. Repairs may have to be made to the space station or to other small satellites. Various experiments may require setting up or observation. The most common need for extra-vehicular activity, or a space walk, will probably be for construction, perhaps of solar electrical power stations or large communications satellites, and so on.

Before going into the vacuum of space, you will have to hook into a special life support system, a suit designed to provide all the elements needed to sustain life—that is, air, temperature control, and radiation protection. Wearing the spacesuit is like being in a small, personalized space station. A main garment covers the torso, arms, and legs. The suit is made up of many individual layers of material. Some, called "vapor shields," prevent air from escaping from the suit. Other layers protect the wearer from radiation and micrometeoroids. Still others provide insulation from heat and cold. Space gloves, boots, and a helmet have an airtight seal with the suit. Because of the sun and solar radiation that can damage one's eyes, a special gold-plated shield can be pulled down over the front of the helmet. This shield must always be used during a space walk.

Although the suit looks bulky, you can move almost as

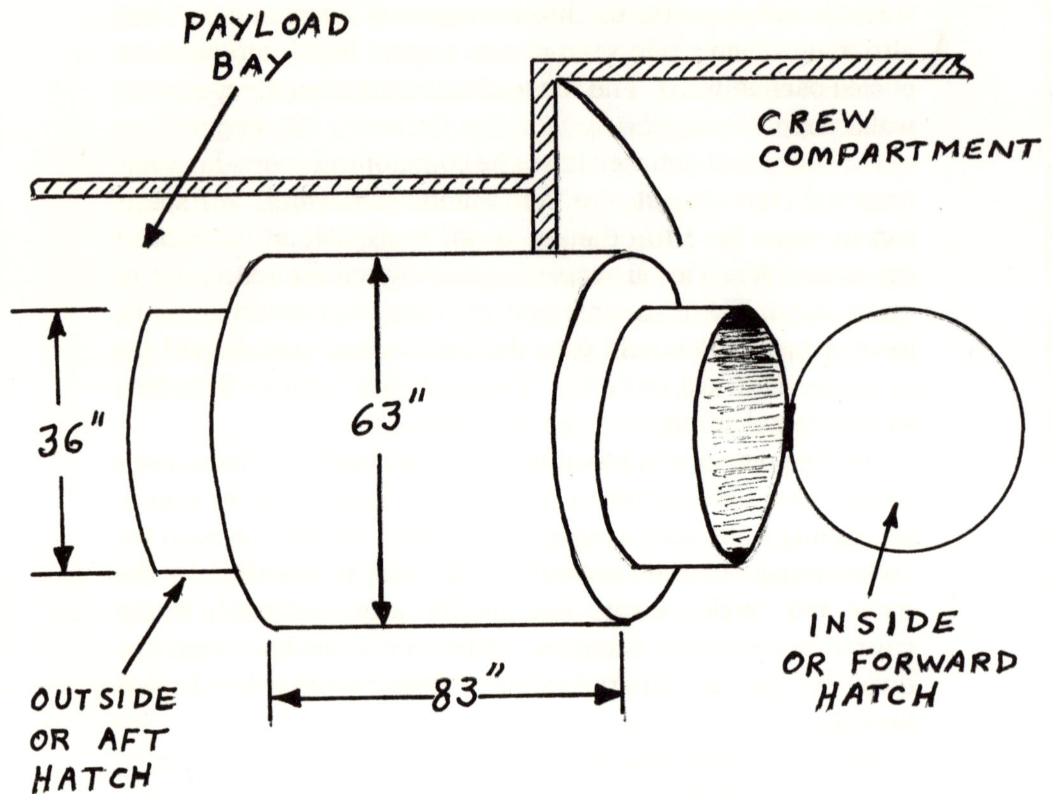

Airlock used to exit and enter the spacecraft so that pressure changes do not affect cabin area when an astronaut has to enter the vacuum of space.

naturally as if the suit were not on. The gloves even have fingernails to allow you to pick up small objects.

In the early years of the space program (Gemini and Apollo), astronauts could make short-distance space walks without a lot of special equipment. They were able to plug themselves into the spacecraft's life support system. But the heavy life support lines were clumsy and did not allow an astronaut to go very far away from the craft. During the moon landing program, astronauts had to travel far from the spacecraft to explore the surface of the moon. When an astronaut cannot rely on the spacecraft or space station's life support system, other equipment must be used: a backpack—built into the suit—which contains all the equipment for keeping alive. The backpack recycles breathing air and removes vapors from the spacesuit.

One very important function of the backpack is to maintain a comfortable temperature in the spacesuit. It does this by pumping cooling water into a series of thin tubes that run through the undergarment of the spacesuit. Body heat is absorbed by the water and carried away, keeping the astronaut cool. If the outside temperature becomes colder—in a shadow area, for example—the circulation process is slowed so that less heat is carried off.

The life support backpack also contains the equipment necessary for the astronaut to communicate with another astronaut, or to the space station, spacecraft, or even back to Earth.

Warning signals, both visual and audible, tell the astronaut when the life support supplies are running low.

With the use of a backpack, a space walker can move a considerable distance away from the spacecraft. On the moon, the astronauts traveled several thousand feet from the craft. In space, however, going too far away from the spacecraft can be dangerous. You can begin to drift and tumble in such a way that you cannot get back to the spacecraft. To prevent you from wandering too far, you are connected to the craft by a tether, a strong nylon cord to pull yourself back to the craft if necessary. You will use a tether even if you have a "hand thruster." This is a miniature hand-held rocket gun that is used to propel you through space.

The equipment needed to support human life gives you an idea of difficulties of living and working in space. There are many problems that face you during your daily routine, problems which make living in space a lot different from living on Earth.

Here Edward H. White II floats into space—the first American to walk in space. He wears an emergency oxygen supply chest pack and is carrying a Hand-Held-Self-Maneuvering unit to help him move about. The tether line is actually an umbilical cord tying him to the vessel's support systems *and* a tether, both wrapped together with gold tape to form a single unit.

Chapter 3

People Problems

Here on Earth, we go about our business giving little thought to our daily routine. We rise after a night's sleep, take a shower or a bath, eat breakfast, walk to school or work, and seldom think about the fact that we are doing all these things. Things are not that easy in space. The simplest tasks can be nerve-racking. Think about washing and taking a shower.

During the days of Mercury, there was no real problem about clean bodies or clothes. Flights were very short and one could go without a shower for a day or two. Even during Gemini, one could manage to stand the minor discomfort of several days without a real shower, and soiled clothing could wait for an earthly laundromat. However, with space flights approaching weeks in duration, washing in space is essential.

At first, the sponge bath was the big thing. But even a simple thing like squeezing the sponge had to be done differently. If you squeeze a sponge in the ordinary way, the fluid gathers into a single glob of moisture and goes floating around the cabin with the slightest motion.

For Skylab, NASA developed a special type of shower. The astronaut steps into a flexible plastic cylinder. After soaping up, the astronaut rinses off using a spray nozzle in one hand while sucking up the water with a vacuum hose in the other. The key here is to remain in a small enclosed area to prevent water and soapsuds from floating around the cabin. Unfortunately, this method of taking a shower is very time-consuming—about 45 minutes. During the Skylab project, some of the astronauts avoided this procedure by rubbing themselves down with damp towels.

You will be using a much-improved method. You might step into a shower stall and lock a tightly sealed door. Then you would press a button drawing a stream of air from overhead. A suction pump beneath the stall would also be turned on so the air would be sucked down into the floor. With this flow established, you would press a second button to turn on the water. The water sprays out of the shower head under pressure and is trapped in the downward stream of air. In this way, you can stand under the shower and wash in the normal way.

Of course, foot restraints are needed to keep you standing up!

Eating presents still another problem in space. Under zero-G (no-gravity) conditions it is not possible to cook in the normal fashion. Food floats out of the pot—or the soup bowl, glass, cup, or plate.

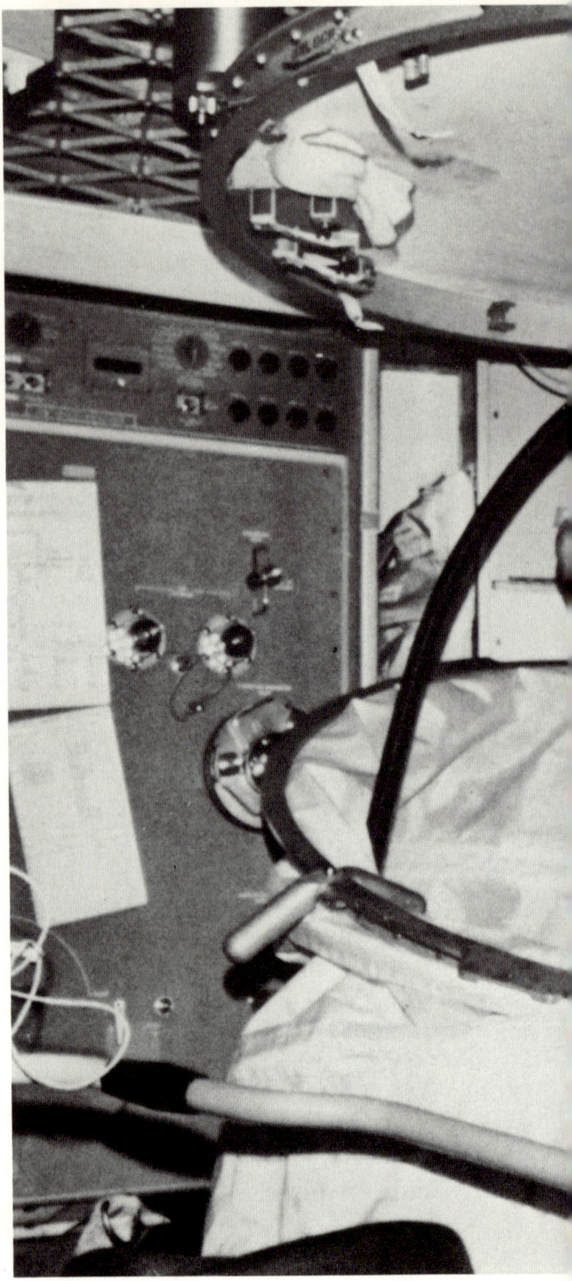

Jack R. Lousma bathing in Skylab space station. The shower curtain is pulled up from the floor and attached to the ceiling.

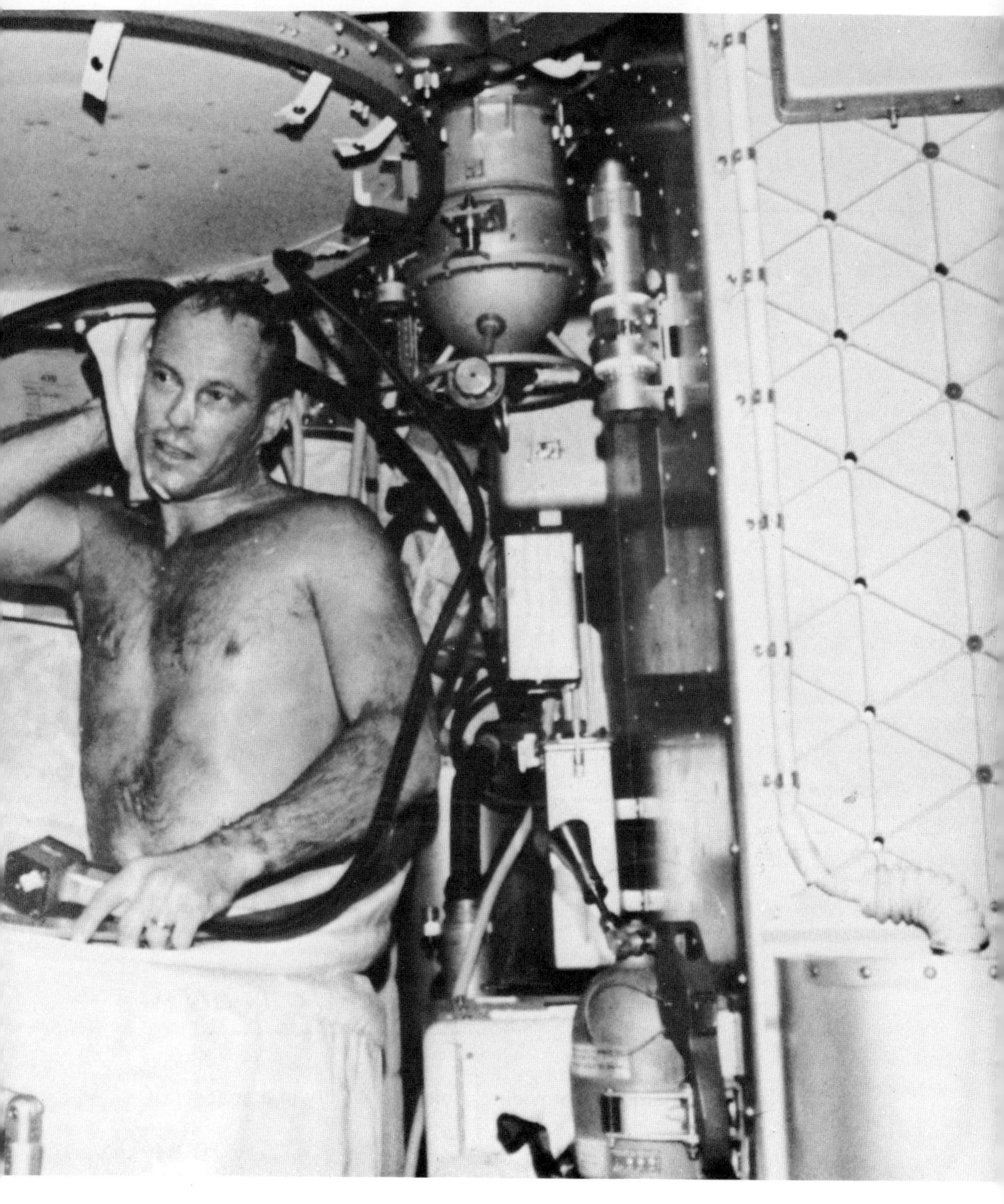

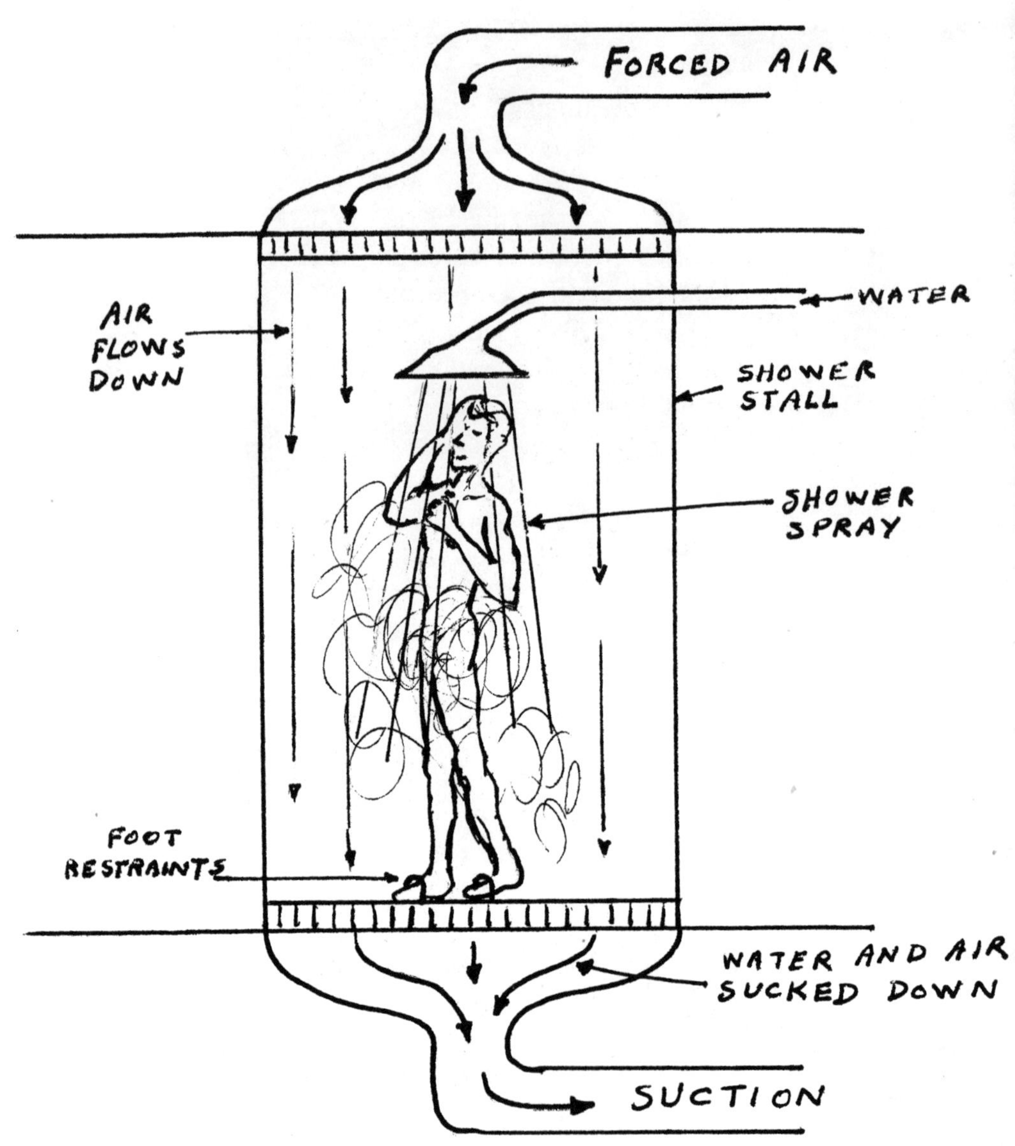

One possible method of providing a shower facility in a spacecraft.

The first astronauts in space had to settle for a rather crude form of eating. Various types of food were provided in paste form in tubes. Or hot water was added to specially freeze-dried foods also in tubes. Astronauts would hold the tube to their mouths, squeeze it, and the food would be forced, like toothpaste, out of the tube and into their mouths. This method was also used for liquids. The astronauts had to be careful to keep their mouths closed, or food would go floating around that could become lodged in some delicate equipment. Or bits of food could be inhaled by one of the crew, causing serious lung irritation.

During the Skylab project, when there was plenty of room for special equipment and food storage, the menu improved. There were facilities for heating solid foods: prime ribs of beef, filet mignon, roast chicken or turkey, and many other appetizing dishes. And while you couldn't eat soup with a spoon, you could use a spoon for puddings and ice cream, which normally cling to a surface by friction. Biscuits and cookies were packaged in wrappers that were eatable, too.

The weightlessness of space creates many other strange problems. One can imagine the problem involved with going to the bathroom in weightless conditions. Aside from the fact that the human body must be held in place using handrails or straps, there is the challenge of the commode itself. An ordinary toilet cannot function in space. NASA had to have a bathroom commode especially designed to compensate for the lack of gravity. The early commodes used air to force waste into a collection bag. The bag was made of a special material that allowed air to pass through but captured solids and liquids. The airflow held the solids and liquids at the bottom of the bag.

To dispose of the bag, the astronaut carefully closed it, removed it from the commode, and placed it in a special waste dryer unit. The bag was then heated to drive the moisture out. The moisture, in the form of vapor, was sucked into space when a small door was opened. But the vapor first passed through a fine filter which captured bacteria and other contaminants. After the bag was dried, it was placed in a trash barrel which was returned to Earth and discarded.

A new, modern version of the space commode has been developed for the space shuttle and for future space stations. It looks very similar to a standard house commode. However, it has separate receptacles in the seat to collect liquids and solids. The new commode will add another touch of the comforts of home to an otherwise alien atmosphere.

Even sleeping is not a natural activity in space. On Earth, when you are tired you lie down and go to sleep. Your head sinks into the pillow and your mind realizes that you have placed your body into a sleeping position. But in a spacecraft or space station, sleep is not that simple.

The problem is you cannot lie down in space. You can close your eyes, but your body, along with your blanket and pillow, would simply float around the cabin. When you want to sleep, you get into a special type of sleeping bag which is connected to a surface—a floor or wall or even a ceiling. A restraining belt is used to press your head against the pillow. It may seem strange to see someone sleeping against a wall or on a ceiling, but that is part of life in space. It takes some getting used to.

There is nothing natural about living in space. Nothing comes easy. Almost everything that is done must be approached in a

Bathroom commode system under study for use in Space Shuttle.

different way. Take a simple thing such as brushing your teeth. You can't just squeeze the tube of paste, or the effort of even such a small movement is liable to start you floating off in the opposite direction. There is no gravity to hold you down. So you have to be strapped down or holding tight onto something when you squeeze the tube. That goes for brushing, too. The force of brushing your teeth could send you twisting and spinning. You also have to be careful to keep your mouth closed while brushing, or globs of paste and saliva will be sent floating around the cabin. So part of an astronaut's training includes the not-so-simple act of brushing the teeth.

Shaving and washing present other problems. Remember, everything floats around in space: water, hair, soap, you. In the early years of space flight, NASA designed a special electric shaver which also contained a small vacuum cleaner. So, as an astronaut shaved, the vacuum sucked up the loose hairs. As it turned out, the astronauts learned that a simple lather and safety razor also worked well. That is because the lather clings to the skin by friction instead of gravity. The lather also holds the hairs once they have been shaved off. Of course, an astronaut has got to be careful not to shake away the lather.

Even getting a haircut has its problems. The cutting of the hair and the collecting of the cut hair must be done together. A vacuum hose closely followed the scissors.

It is also more difficult for astronauts to hear each other talking in a space station. That is because the atmosphere of 5 pounds per square inch is much thinner than Earth's 15 pounds per square inch. The thinner air doesn't allow sound to travel very well. Dr. Joseph Kerwin, an astronaut on the Skylab project, explained that he and the other men were hoarse all the time from shouting at one another to be heard. He also complained that the thin atmosphere made it very difficult to whistle!

It is a problem just to walk—one step and the astronaut may float and tumble across the cabin. On Skylab, magnetic shoes made it possible for the astronauts to walk across a metal floor.

The absence of gravity in space poses another serious problem to astronauts who spend long periods of time away from the surface of our planet.

Here on Earth, gravity is always exerting a certain amount of force on our bodies. Gravity pulls us against the surface of the Earth. In response to this force, our muscles work to keep us standing up. Our muscles work to support our bodies. Our hearts work hard to pump blood uphill from our feet and arms, away from the pull of gravity.

In space, no force of gravity is acting on the body. It is much easier for the heart to pump blood, and for blood to return to the heart from the lower part of the body. Muscles relax since they do not have to work against the force of gravity—in fact, they relax so much that if you are in space for a long time, you grow in height. It is possible to actually grow an inch or more in space because, as the muscles relax, the joints of the body separate a little.

All this may sound like a good thing, but it is not. Under weightless conditions, our muscles, including our heart muscles, get lazy. After a while without having to work hard, they begin to get weak.

Special equipment and a routine of exercises for flight crews is essential to protect bodies from the physical effects of weightlessness. Astronauts obviously cannot use weights to exercise. A 500-pound dumbbell would merely float around the cabin. So

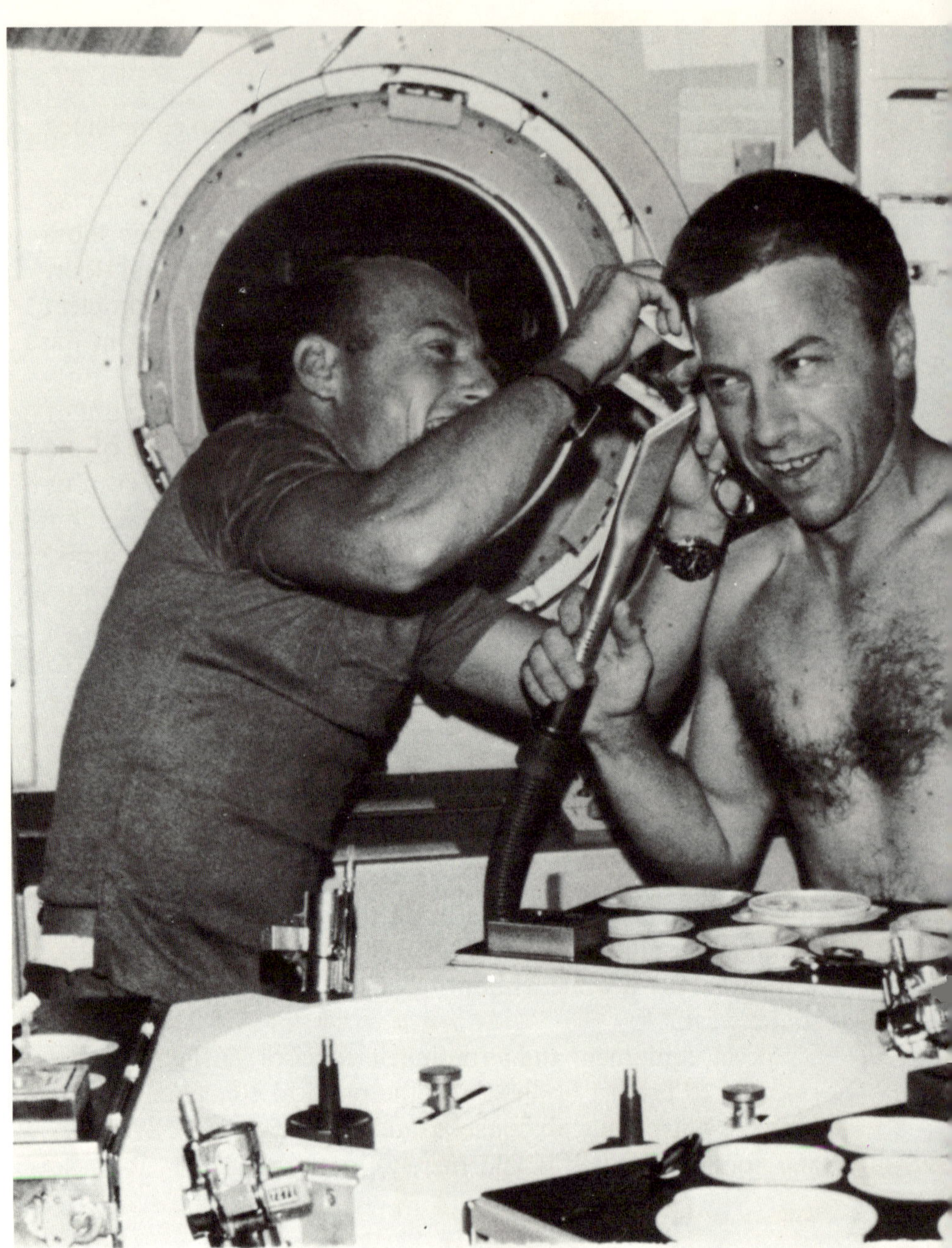

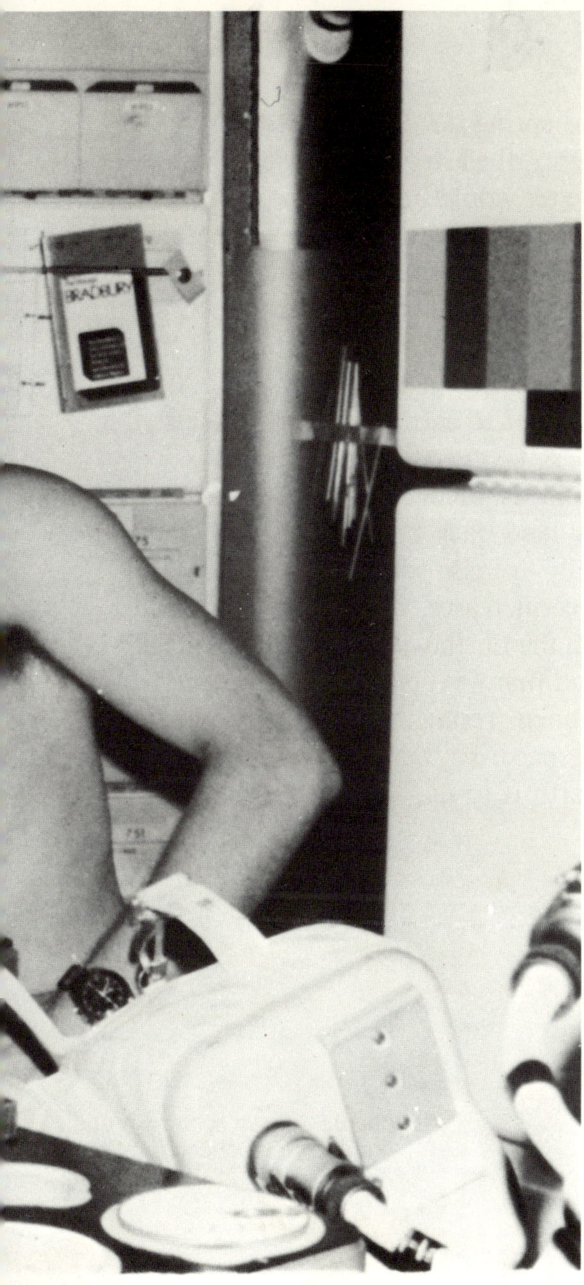

Charles Conrad, Jr. trims the hair of Paul J. Weitz during 28-day Skylab 2 mission. Astronaut Weitz is following the clippers with a vacuum hose.

bicycle exercise machines and spring devices are used.

During the long Skylab flights, the astronauts learned that the more exercise they got, the better would be their condition when they returned to Earth. The crew of the first flight exercised for about 45 minutes each day of the month-long journey. During the second flight, which lasted twice as long, they exercised for over an hour each day. On the third flight, 3 months long, the astronauts exercised for an hour and a half every day. As it turned out, the third crew returned to earth in the best condition of all.

Russian astronauts who hold the record for time in space are strong and steady when they land back on Earth. That is only possible with a strenuous daily exercise schedule.

As our knowledge of space increases, most of the common problems of living away from the Earth will be solved. Artificial gravity will enable us to spend many years in space. Communities will one day have permanent residence in the sky. People will spend their entire lives in space. To them, living in space will be as natural as living on Earth is to us.

Astronauts Joseph P. Kerwin and Paul J. Weitz check out their bike exerciser.

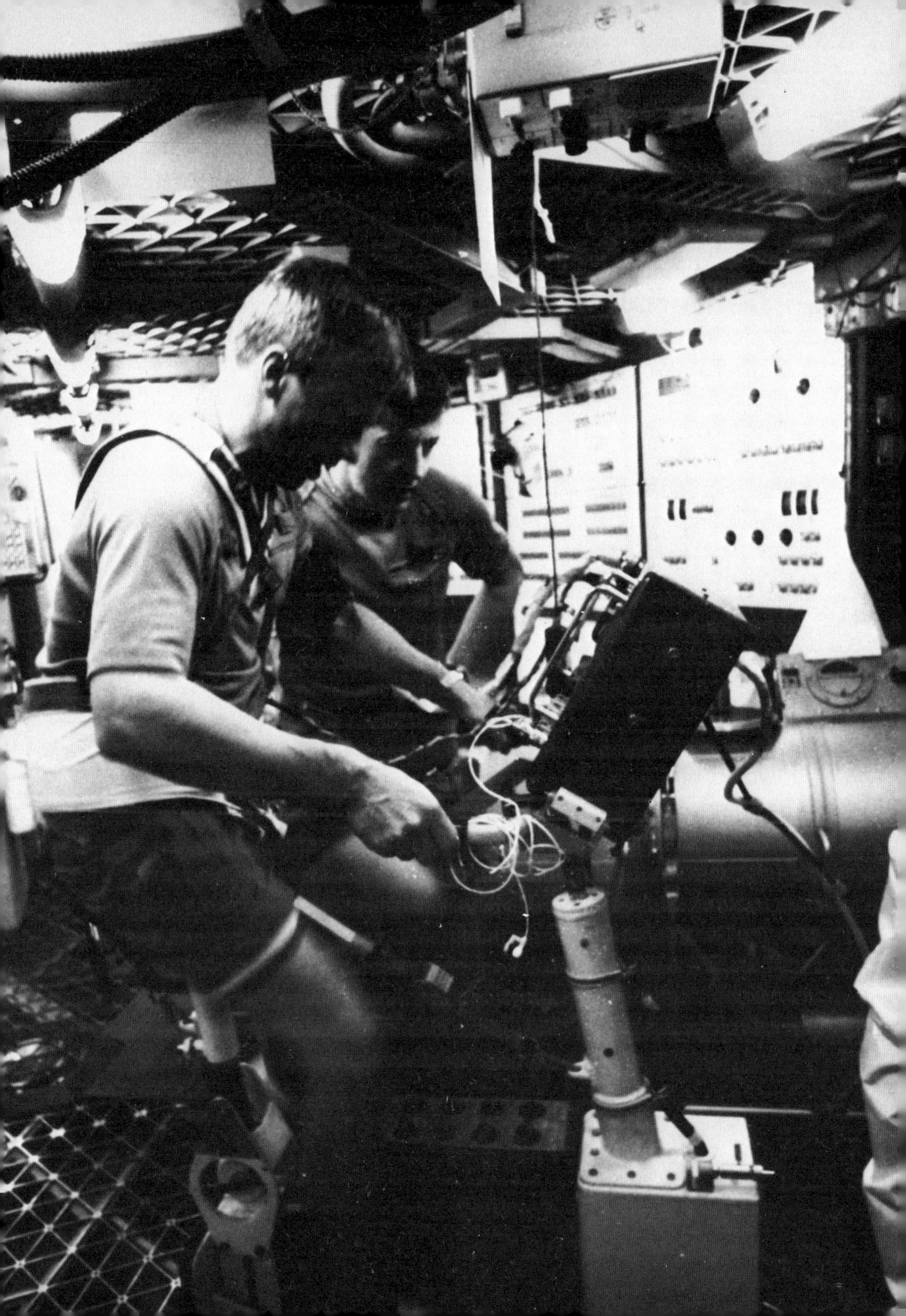

Chapter 4

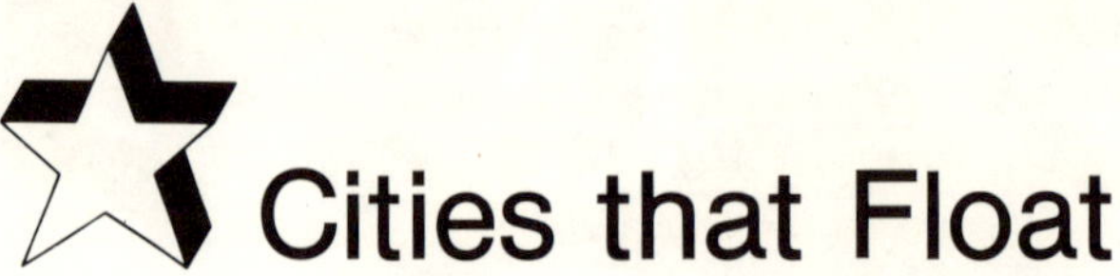

Cities that Float

Space is a severe challenge to human life. But most scientists believe that people can live permanently in space. Scientists would provide artificial gravity. There would also have to be new scientific breakthroughs in life support systems, agriculture, manufacturing, and other areas before we could build places in space where large numbers of people could live permanently.

But we have already come a long way toward that goal. It was not very long ago—May 5, 1961—when Alan B. Shepard, Jr., became the first American to enter space. He did not go into orbit, and his flight, in a small Mercury capsule, lasted only 15 minutes. But only 5 years later, project Gemini proved that 2 men could live in space for up to 2 weeks. By 1973, the United States placed a scientific laboratory in space, Skylab, in which 3 astronauts spent 85 days working, eating, exercising, and conducting research.

Skylab I was a giant structure for its time. About the size of a large house, the space station weighed 200,000 pounds and contained 13,000 cubic feet of space in which to live and work. Skylab had large solar power wings, a huge telescope, an airlock, and it was connected to the Apollo spacecraft. It was a giant step away from the lonely little Mercury capsule of only a decade past.

Scientists are confident that people can remain in space for extended periods of time. Dr. Gerald K. O'Neill of Princeton University has designs for a giant structure in space that will allow thousands of people to live in Earth orbit permanently. It is also possible that there will be cities on the moon or even on Mars.

We will have to start small at first and work our way up to a full-sized colony. The establishment of a permanent city in the sky will be accomplished in a series of steps. The first step will probably be a modest space station with a crew of about 12 to 20. In 1970, North American Rockwell and the McDonnell Douglas Aircraft Corporation made a multi-million-dollar study of how a space station of this size should be designed. They recommended a 4-level space station with a "basement" and an "attic" with over 28,000 cubic feet of living and working space designed to last at least 10 years. The crew of the space station would spend 6 months at a time in the station. However, there might be scientists who would visit the station for only a week or two of special work. A technician might hop aboard a shuttle on

An artist's conception of a Satellite Power System construction. Such a weblike structure would collapse on Earth. In space, this would be covered with thousands of solar cells which convert sunlight to electricity.

JOHN J. OLSON

a Monday morning, arrive at the space station, and put in a week's work. He or she would be home again on the following Saturday.

Once at the station, a scientist would have a busy schedule, working 10 hours a day, 6 days a week. The remainder of each day would be carefully scheduled: 2½ hours for eating and 1 hour for personal hygiene, and about 2½ hours each day for special exercise to keep in shape for the return trip to Earth and normal gravity. That leaves 8 hours for sleep and whatever recreational activities can be fitted in.

Let's take a brief tour of the station. The lowest portion of the structure, the basement, is where we'll find the noisy hardware—the pumps, fans, and valves—the fuel and water storage tanks, supplies, and some control equipment.

In the center of the station is a 5-foot-wide tunnel, or corridor, which runs through the entire structure. This is the main thoroughfare for all levels. We use this passageway to get to the first level, called Deck 1.

On Deck 1 we find the galley (kitchen) and the wardroom (meeting room). Deck 1 also contains the medical room, which is used as a first-aid station and for research. Even though there are all these areas, there is a feeling of roominess since the decks are 33 feet in diameter.

Next we go to Deck 2. Here we find staterooms (bedrooms) for 5 crew members and the station commander. Each room is comfortable, not cramped. There's a bed, a work area, a television set, and a communications device for a crew member to place calls, even to Earth. And there are enough bathrooms so that no one has to stand in line.

Deck 2 also contains the primary control center for the space station. Here we find the on-board checkout system which keeps an eye on all the space station equipment and alerts the crew if anything goes wrong. The crew does not have to rely on ground control to monitor the station 24 hours a day.

Deck 3 has rooms for another 6 of the crew. It also has more bathrooms, an experimental area, and back-up controls for the station. If pressurization were lost on Decks 1 and 2, the crew could remain on Deck 3 and control the station.

Deck 4 is devoted to experiments. Here we find all the electronic, biological, and physics equipment to perform dozens of types of experiments in medicine, communications, and space manufacturing. Deck 4 also contains a photographic laboratory.

The attic, or upper deck, contains the same kind of bulky, noisy equipment found in the basement.

What would such an installation cost? About $10 billion. And it would require a great deal of expensive support equipment. For example, at least 3 shuttles are needed to support the activities of the station. One shuttle would be at the station, a second one being prepared for its next flight, and a third just returning from the station. A constant supply of materials and equipment are needed to maintain the crew and station in operation.

It is surprising how much food and general supplies are required to support a full crew in a space station. Over the course of a year, a typical person consumes 3 times his or her body weight in food, 4 times his or her weight in oxygen, and 8 times his or her weight in drinking water. So for a 6-month tour for a crew member weighing 178 pounds, here is what would be required: 263 pounds of food, 385 pounds of oxygen, and 788 pounds of drinking water: a total of 1,436 pounds of consumables. Add to this about 1,000 pounds of sanitary water to shower and wash clothes, and we've got over a ton of weight per person.

Then there are the other items such as clothes, books, films, games, medicines, and maintenance items such as filters, seals, and so on, and the weight of supplies really adds up. It is roughly estimated that shuttles will carry about 12,000 pounds of cargo up to the station each month and carry back about 7,000 pounds to Earth. And we're only talking about a 12-person space station.

The space station also needs a large supply of electrical power. Most of the power would be supplied by solar power panels. Skylab required about 32,000 watts of electricity. A 12-person station will require perhaps 3 times that amount to support all of its experiments and other activities.

All the materials needed to build a solar power station (SPS) or space colony—tons of aluminum, titanium, silicon, and other materials—could be carried up from Earth. But that could create an environmental problem. The rockets needed to carry the materials into space would pour many millions of tons of polluting exhaust gases into the atmosphere every year. However, there are other places where we would get the raw materials for the projects—the moon, for instance.

Artist's conception of Space Shuttle.

esa
USA

The lunar surface is rich in the things we need, like aluminum and titanium for electrical cables and beams and girders. About 20 percent of the lunar surface is silicon. Silicon is needed to make the solar cells which produce electricity when sunlight shines on them. Oxygen from the moon would be used for rocket fuel, would be combined with hydrogen to make water, and it would be a major ingredient of the atmosphere for a space colony.

Of course, the big question is, how do we get all that material from the surface of the moon to our construction site in space?

One possibility would be to use large freighter-type spacecrafts. But this would be very expensive. There is a better and cheaper way to get the material there: the "mass driver."

The mass driver consists of a number of buckets moved by magnetic force. Magnets called "acceleration coils" are mounted on a track designed to carry a series of buckets. The buckets are filled with lunar material. Then a button is pressed, sending a surge of electricity through the first acceleration coil. This creates a magnetic field which slowly pulls the bucket forward. Once the bucket arrives at the first coil, the electricity is cut off and then sent through the second coil. A strong magnetic field is created around the second coil. The bucket, moving more quickly, is pulled forward to the second coil. Then the third coil pulls the bucket forward, increasing its speed still

Lunar mass driver.

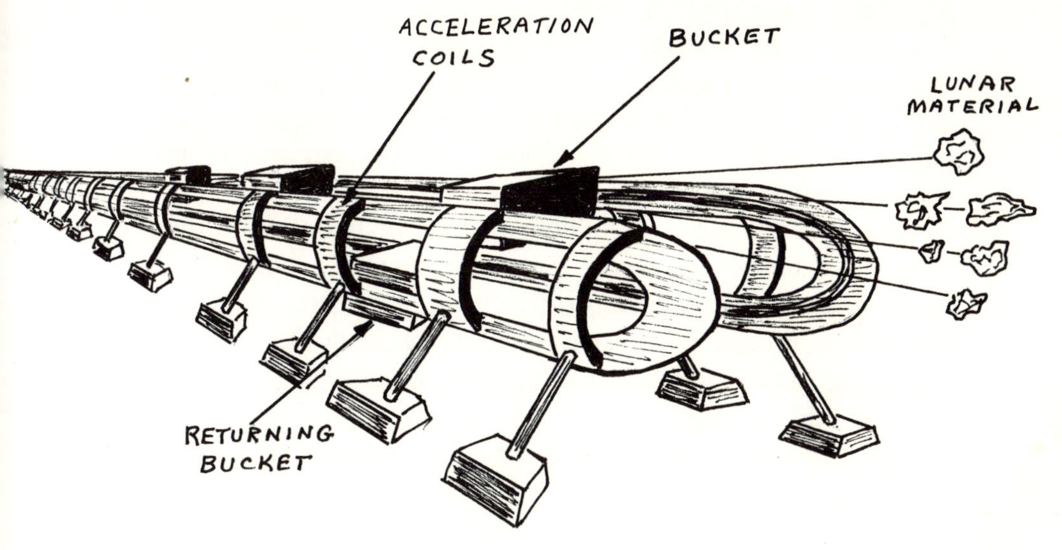
ACCELERATION
COILS
BUCKET
LUNAR
MATERIAL
RETURNING
BUCKET

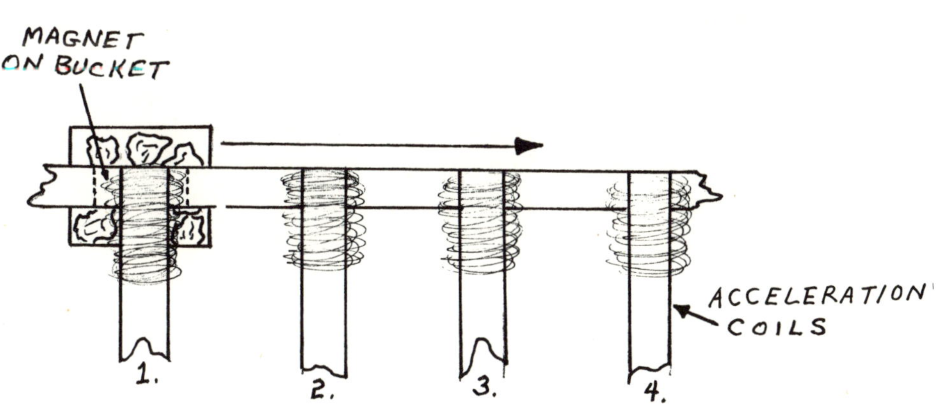
MAGNET
ON BUCKET
ACCELERATION
COILS
1.
2.
3.
4.

more. The bucket continues to pick up speed as it moves along thousands of acceleration coils, until it and its load of rocks are moving at a tremendous speed.

Suddenly, the bucket is stopped. But the material in the bucket keeps traveling, because nothing is holding the load in. The front of the bucket is open and all the material goes flying out at top speed. That speed is about 7,500 feet per second, the escape speed from the pull of moon gravity.

Well, here we are with millions of tons of material hurtling through space. Now what? Stopping tons of rocks flying through space sounds terribly difficult. In fact, it sounds almost impossible. But scientists have found a way to do it.

Located in the general area of the SPS or colony construction site is an odd-looking structure called a "mass catcher." A mass catcher is essentially a huge plastic bag in a metal frame with a large circular rim or mouth. A number of steel cables crisscross the mouth. When the lunar rocks reach the catcher, they smash against the cables and break into small pieces and are captured in the plastic bag.

This system of transporting materials from the moon to our space colony is fairly simple after all.

And just where is that space colony?

You may think that space is the same all over and that it does not matter where a space colony is located. That's not so. Let's say a large structure is placed in a close, or low, orbit (circular path) around the earth. The space shuttle would be able to reach the station easily. However, because of the effects of the earth's atmosphere, a low-orbit colony would slowly be pulled back to Earth. In other words, a low Earth orbit is very unstable. So where do we place the colony?

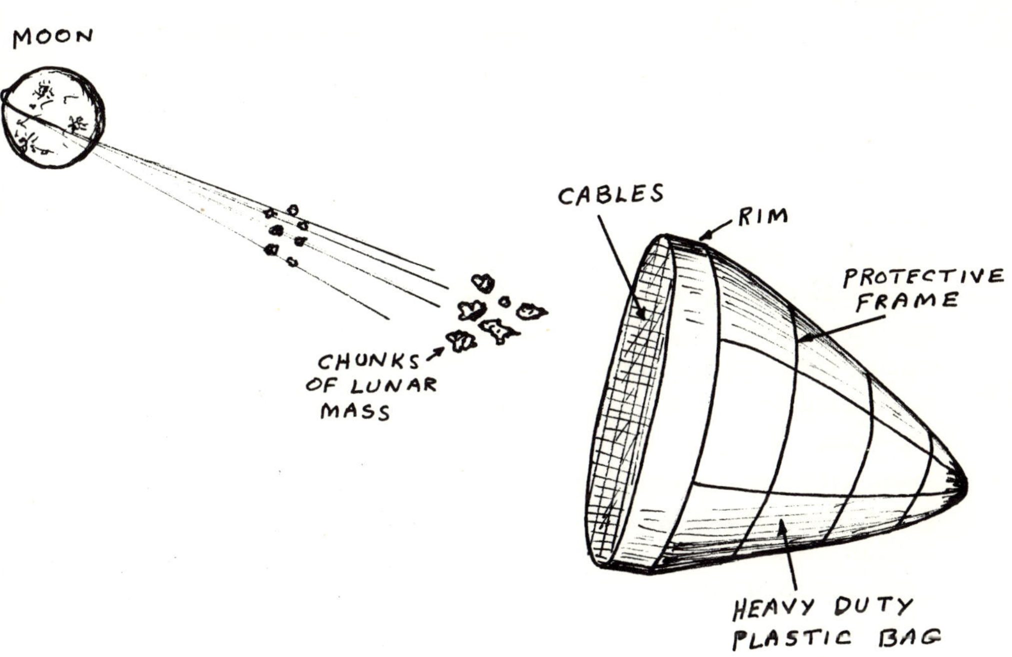

Mass catcher.

Astronomers tell us that there are areas in our Earth/moon system that are very stable. They go by the very fancy name of "lagrangian libration points." These are points in space where the moon's gravity is equal in pull to the Earth's gravity. Therefore, a structure at this point will not be pulled back to Earth *or* toward the moon.

Our space colony will be situated at a langrangian libration point called L5. L5 is about 250,000 miles from Earth and the same distance from the moon. Once in place, the colony will remain in the L5 area for millions of years.

Now that a location for a space colony has been chosen, what next?

One of the most serious of challenges to the designers of our space colony is the danger of radiation. Radiation is probably the single most serious problem for space travelers. The exposure to large amounts of radiation is deadly to human beings.

There are two main sources of radiation in the space around the Earth—the sun, and the galaxy in which we live.

Normally, the radiation from the sun does not affect humans seriously because it can be avoided. But solar flares, storms on the sun, send showers of deadly types of radiation across space with little warning.

Then there are the super-powerful rays from the galaxy. Without adequate protection, a person would receive about 20 times the maximum allowable radiation from these cosmic rays. Here on Earth, nature has provided us with a natural protective shield, the atmosphere that surrounds us. But in space, that protection must take another form: the shield must be built into the structure.

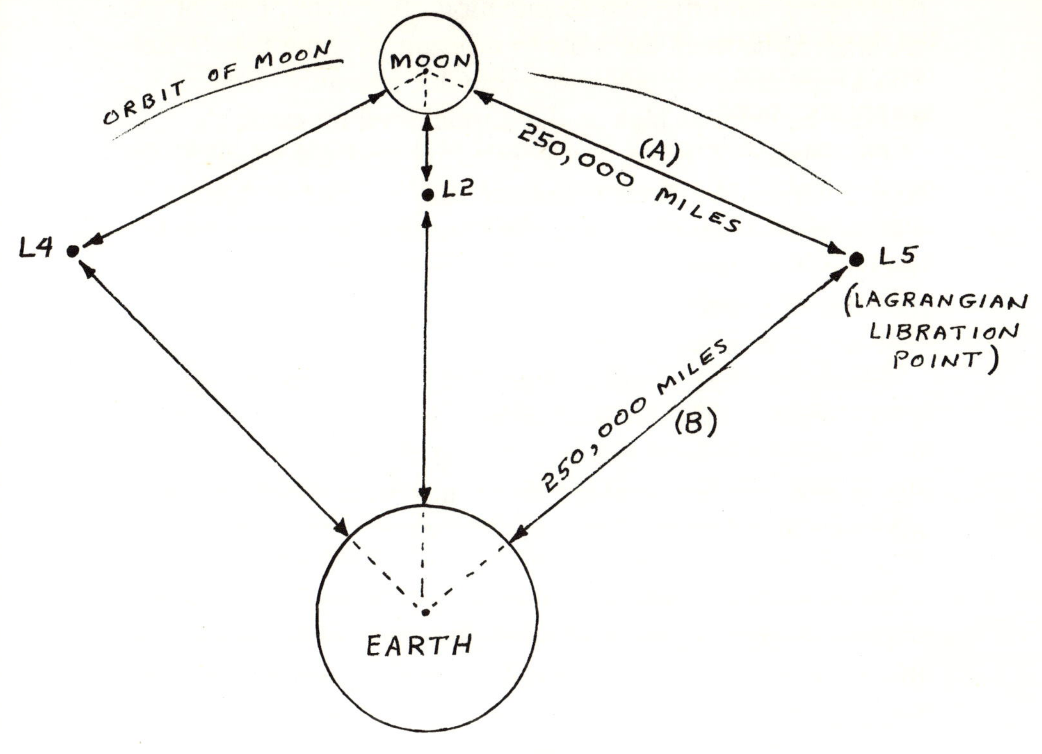

A new homeland in space.

Space colonies might have a double shell, an inner and outer hull as in a ship. This double-walled structure is still not capable of stopping powerful cosmic radiation. To do this, bags of soil are stacked between the hulls to a height of more than 7 feet. This keeps radiation down to acceptable amounts—although it will still be twice as high as the normal level on earth.

This means of protection is primitive and not practical for large colonies. We already have an idea of what such colonies will be like—scientists such as Dr. Gerald O'Neill have worked out plans for a typical colony of hundreds of thousands, or even millions, of people.

It would be quite a sight.

Imagine a tube measuring about 500 feet thick being bent into a huge wheel. In the center of the wheel is a large hub connected to the wheel rim by 6 spokes. Floating above the rim is a large flat mirror reflecting sunlight down into the central hub. Other mirrors will reflect this light into the wheel.

In the colony everything will operate on electricity—heating, cooling, cooking, and transportation will all run on electricity.

Once inside, a visitor will be dumbstruck by the vastness of the colony: trees, patios, schools, shopping centers, theaters, small farms, roads, swimming pools—everything one might find on Earth. But there is one big difference. Everything in the colony—everything—is fully controlled. The weather, temperature, humidity, length of day and night—everything is under the control of computers.

Each person is allotted about 360 square feet of living space. That would be an area 18 feet by 20 feet, roughly the size of a large room. But that does not include height. Therefore, a family of 3 could have three levels of space, or 3 x 360 square feet. A family of 4 could have 4 times that space.

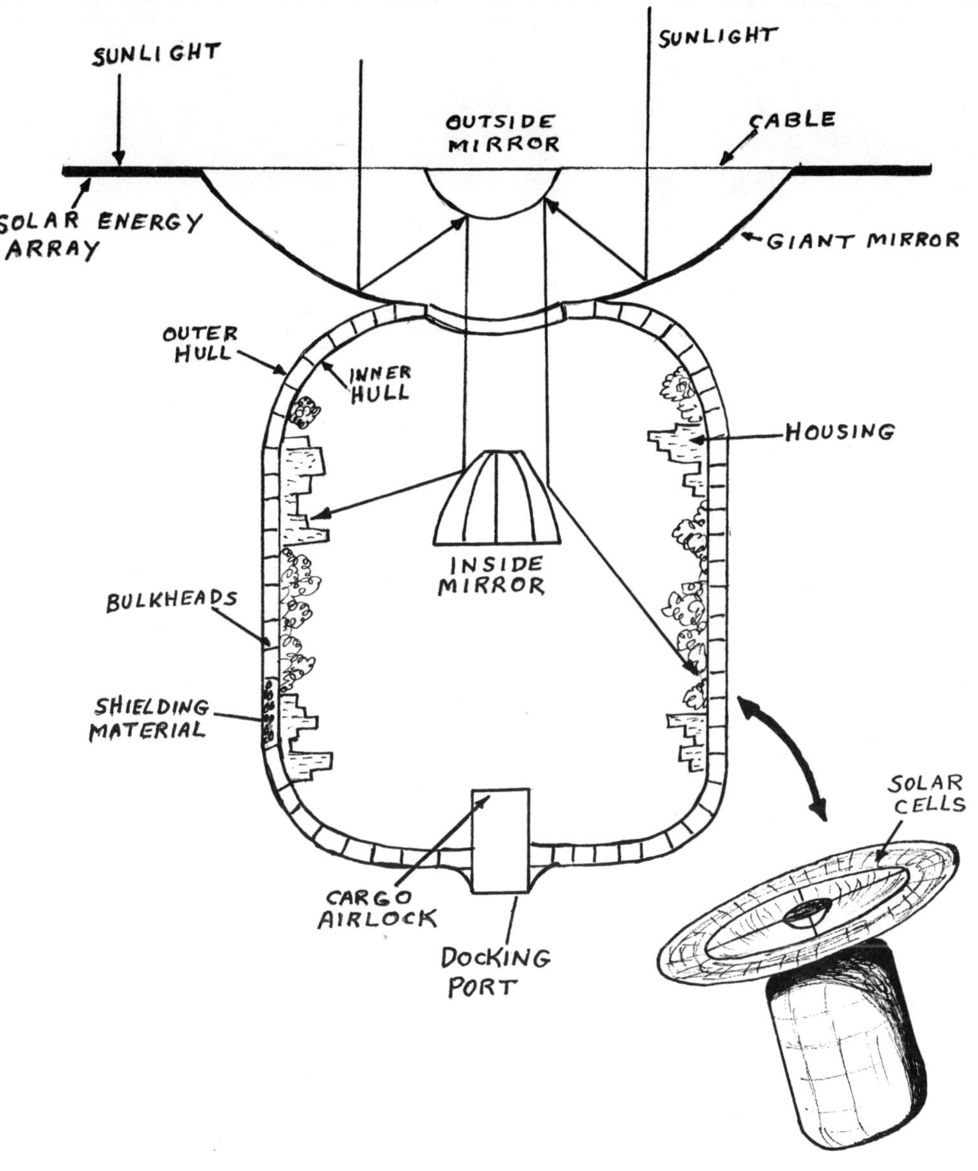

An MIT team designed this space colony to support 1,000 inhabitants.

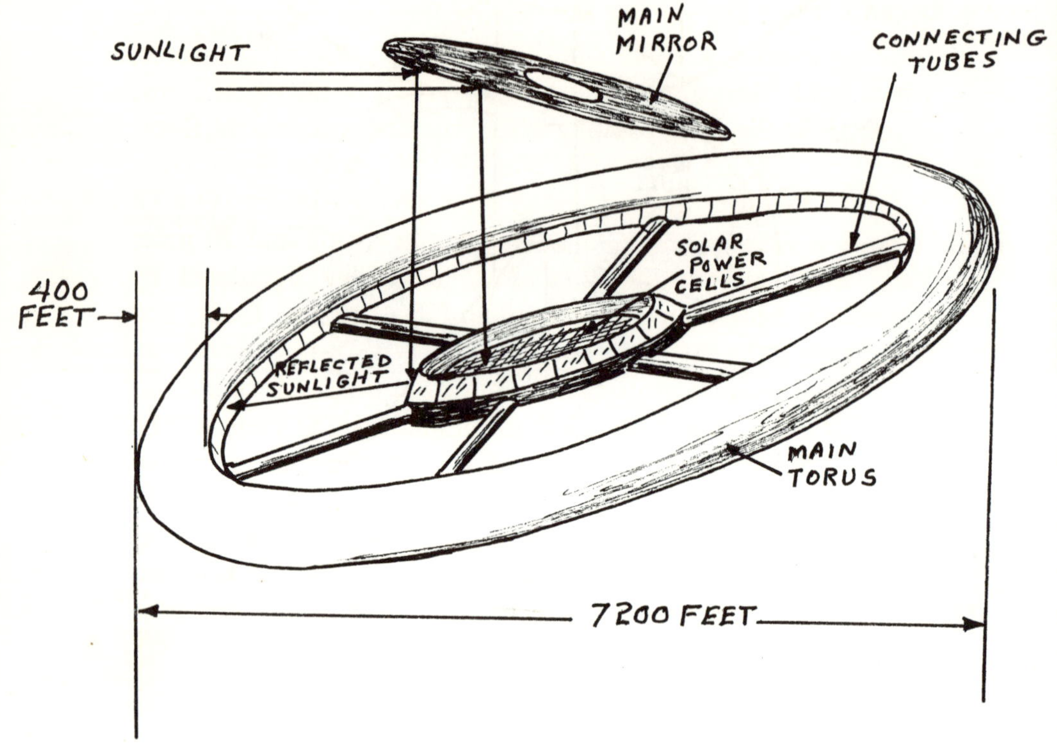

Another design for a permanent space structure to house colonists in space.

But we can't have all these thousands of people floating around in a giant wheel. So the scientists will introduce artificial gravity. They will do this by rotating the entire structure. The rotation creates a force similar to gravity, centrifugal force, which holds everything against the side walls of the wheel. Now, if you are in this large rotating wheel, the sides become the floor. The force holding you to the "floor" feels exactly like gravity.

Dr. O'Neill has also suggested other colony designs. One of these is a giant cylinder, measurig 4 miles wide and 20 miles long. Such an enormous structure could be populated by 20,000,000 people and could contain hills, streams, fields, and many trees.

The cost of such projects is estimated at hundreds of billions of dollars. But eventually all this will happen and there will be generations of people who will call a huge structure in the sky their homeland. They will in fact be extraterrestrial life, life forms outside of Earth. If it is possible for us to be extraterrestrial, isn't it possible that somewhere else in the heavens, among those countless stars, there are other extraterrestrials?

Chapter 5

Aliens

The great popularity of television shows and movies such as *Star Trek, Battlestar Galactica, Star Wars, Close Encounters of the Third Kind* and others has aroused a great curiosity in people about alien life among the distant star systems. Is there any intelligent life outside of Earth?

This is one of the more difficult questions facing scientists today. They have not found any life yet, but they are making an intensive search. It must occur to anyone surveying the countless stars that perhaps someone, somewhere in the endless sky, might be looking back at us.

Furious arguments concerning the question of extraterrestrial life were started in 1893 by the Italian astronomer Giovanni Schiaparelli. After conducting a study of Mars by telescope, he announced that canals could be seen on the red planet. Schiaparelli suggested that they were the work of intelligent inhabitants. A debate raged in the scientific world over the subject for years. In 1908, astronomer Percival Lowell published a book entitled *Mars as the Abode of Life.* He was thoroughly convinced that the canals were constructed by intelligent beings and openly proclaimed that creatures "alike to us in spirit, though not in form" lived on Mars. Naturally, attempts to communicate with our planetary neighbors were immediately launched.

One experiment involved the use of searchlights. Coded messages were beamed toward Mars in the hopes that its inhabitants would respond to our invitation to communicate. But public interest soon faded and so did funds for such projects.

But a half-century later came Sputnik (1957), and once again all eyes were on the heavens.

In 1960, the scientific community, under the leadership of Dr. Frank Drake, started an extraterrestrial life-search program named OZMA, after Dorothy's mythical city of Oz. They concentrated on listening for radio signals from 2 nearby stars: Epsilon Eridani and Tau Ceti, located about 11 light-years from Earth. The search lasted for a number of weeks, with no startling results.

The year 1972 saw the start of a couple of large SETI (Search for ExtraTerrestrial Intelligence) programs. An Orbiting Astronomical Observatory (OAO-3) was successfully placed in an Earth orbit and used, on a part-time basis, to search for life. It scanned the stars Epsilon Eridani and Tau Ceti and more distant stars. No life was found.

Project OZMA II was initiated in 1972. About 700 stars were examined in the second OZMA project which was completed in December, 1976, with no real success.

In 1973, Ohio State University got into the life-search act and has been continuously searching the sky for signals, 24 hours a day. Then, Canada's Algonquin Radio Observatory began to examine hundreds of stars for evidence of intelligent life. The giant 1,000-foot dish antenna at Aricebo, Puerto Rico, was used to search for signals from space in a project headed by Drs. Frank Drake and Carl Sagan. The scientists searched the entire Milky Way galaxy for signs of life—unsuccessfully.

We have heard of hundreds of UFO sightings. But no concrete evidence has ever substantiated their presence.

All the scientific searching so far has not provided any evidence that intelligent life exists outside of Earth.

So why are scientists so confident that it is only a matter of time before we become aware of another intelligent civilization?

First of all, sheer numbers suggest the existence of alien societies. Our galaxy, the Milky Way is estimated to have from 100 billion to 400 billion stars. Of these billions of stars, scientists feel that even a very small percentage must have planets revolving around them, as our star, the Sun, does. They feel there may be as few as 200 million and as many as 10 billion planetary systems in our galaxy. And a number of these planets could very well have conditions similar to earth. Suppose we consider that only the minimum 200 million planetary systems exist, and of these, only 1 percent have Earthlike conditions. That means that there are 2 million Earthlike planets in the galaxy. If only 1 in 1,000 of these planets have life, that would give us 2,000 life-bearing planets in the galaxy. Going to the extreme, let us say that only 1 percent of these 2,000 planets had

Just under 100 feet in diameter, this huge dish antenna in Thailand tracks satellites and space-ships. The Aricebo antenna being used to search for intelligent life in space is ten times this size.

advanced civilizations; then we would be down to 200 intelligent civilizations in our galaxy. This is considered an extremely conservative estimate. And it considers only our own galaxy.

Now consider the fact that there are about 200 billion galaxies in the universe. If the percentages were applied to these galaxies, there would then be about 4 trillion intelligent societies in the universe. That is a pretty good population. But remember, these are only scientific theories.

There is no *direct* evidence to support these theories. But there is indirect evidence. For one thing, there is evidence that other planetary systems do exist. Over a period of many years, astronomers have studied the movement of certain stars. They can tell that these stars do not travel in smooth circular paths. Something is causing them to wobble. Scientists say this means that a planet might be orbiting around the star. The powerful pull of gravity exerted by large celestial bodies such as planets could be making these stars wobble.

Our telescopes are not powerful enough to see if a planet actually exists at stellar distances. So scientists can only measure how much a star wobbles, then estimate the size that a planet would have to be to cause that amount of wobble. The best example of wobble is Barnard's Runaway Star, located 6 light-years from Earth. Measurements show a very large companion planet and perhaps a number of planets orbiting Barnard's Star.

Then there are chemicals in interstellar space, the space between the stars, to support the possibility of extraterrestrial life. Life as we know it is based on the availability of certain chemical building blocks. They are hydrogen, oxygen, nitrogen, and, most important, carbon.

All life known to us is carbon-based. The other elements—hydrogen, oxygen, and nitrogen—are required to form an atmosphere and to combine with carbon atoms. Combinations of atoms make molecules, and living organisms are series of complex molecules that react with each other. Until the 1950s, most astronomers considered interstellar space a cold void—certainly no place where complex chemicals could develop and survive. But new types of electronic radio telescopes changed that view quickly. Radio astronomers have since identified 40 different chemical molecules. It is now obvious that interstellar space is rich in the chemicals necessary for life.

There is still more evidence to support the extraterrestrial life theory. Comets that have crashed into the Earth have been studied and found to contain a large number of life-forming chemicals. Some scientists think that comets may have brought life to our Earth. When the comets crashed, they might have seeded Earth with an assortment of extremely simple life forms. These evolved into more complex forms over a period of millions of years. Scientists think that this process may very well have occurred in many other planetary systems than ours.

However, not all scientists are convinced that there are other societies in our galaxy or in other parts of the universe. There are some scientists who feel there does not have to be intelligent life in other parts of the universe simply because life exists on Earth. For example, Dr. Michael H. Hart of Trinity University in San Antonio, Texas, believes it is possible that our earthly civilization may be unique. We may be the only intelligent life form in the universe. After an intensive computer study, Dr. Hart concluded that our civilization is extremely rare, and may be one of a kind. He explains that according to his computer analysis, the estimates of scientists regarding how many planetary systems could support intelligent life are between 100 and 1,000 times too high.

Dr. Hart further points out that extremely rare conditions must exist for a planet to generate life. A star must not be too bright or it will burn up developing life on an orbiting planet. If a star is too small, it forces its planet to orbit very closely and keep one face always pointing toward it. This would evaporate or dry up the atmosphere on one side while freezing the atmosphere on the other. Furthermore, a star must maintain a stable rate of burning for at least 3.7 billion years for life to develop. The Earth barely made it. If it had been only a little closer to the sun, the Earth would have had a 900°F. surface temperature, like Venus. On the other hand, if the Earth were only 1 percent farther away from the sun, our globe would have become a barren desert, like Mars.

Dr. Hart makes one strong point: with all the searches that have been made, not a single bit of conclusive evidence has ever been found—not one signal or a single organism—to support the theory that extraterrestrial life exists. But many other scientist say this could be because the instruments we are using are just not big enough or powerful enough. A group of scientists is working to remedy that situation. One project, Project Cyclops, named after the mythical one-eyed giant, is connecting 1,000 antennae to each other to make one huge 3-mile antenna. Project Cyclops will be able to detect even extremely weak signals from distant corners of the universe.

Aside from waiting to be contacted by our neighbors, we are also letting the rest of the universe know that we're here. As though stranded on a remote island, scientists have sent out messages in satellites and deep-space probes.

In 1972 and 1973, Pioneer deep-space probes arced across interplanetary space, past Jupiter and Saturn and then out of the solar system into interstellar space. The spacecrafts were designed to give us a first close-up look at the planets, but they are also acting as a messenger to the stars. Attached to the surface of each spacecraft is a gold-plated aluminum plaque about the size of this page. Etched into the plaque is a picture of a man and a woman and of our solar system, and other simple coded messages. Of course, it will take about 80,000 years before the spacecrafts arrive at the nearest star to deliver our message.

When two Voyager spacecrafts were launched in 1977, they also headed for Jupiter, Saturn, and Uranus. They were packed with the latest scientific instruments, but they also carried other interesting cargo—different types of Earth messages. This time it was a copper phonograph record with a cartridge and a diamond needle. The record is titled "Sounds of Earth." An aluminum container also holds instructions on how to play the record.

The specially designed 12-inch disc, which operates at 16⅔ r.p.m., contains 120 minutes of information. There are Earth greetings in 55 languages, samples of different types of music, plus the natural sounds of things like sea surf, wind, thunder, birds, whales, dogs, and volcanoes. Also included are messages written in simple code from President Jimmy Carter and Secretary General Kurt Waldheim of the United Nations. The record also contains photographs and scientific information.

Eventually, the Pioneer spacecrafts will leave our solar system and head for the stars, like a bottle in an infinite sea. Who can tell when and where the message will be retrieved? And if it is, what will be the reaction of a remote civilization?

Meanwhile, scientists have also been searching for extraterrestrial life in our own backyard: the moon and Mars. An intensive search of the moon's material has shown that life does not exist there now, nor has it existed in the past. All the lunar samples brought back to earth were carefully inspected for any signs of life—none existed.

Scientists have also looked to Mars for life. An exciting project called Viking sent an automated laboratory to the surface of the red planet. One of the main problems is knowing what to look for. Scientists are not certain what form extraterrestrial life might take.

According to Viking project scientists, any of 4 classes of life forms might be encountered there:

- Class I—organisms requiring high temperatures and a lot of water. These might be earthlike, but unfortunately there would be few times when such conditions ever existed on Mars.

- Class II—organisms that are capable of living in low temperatures but need a lot of water. They might be creatures that are active at night, when the temperature of Mars falls and humidity rises.

Artist's version of Mars lander on the surface of the red planet. The lander is a miniature laboratory packed in a box 59 inches across and 18 inches high. It weighs about a ton. A soil sampler extends at center, and the turret-like structures are cameras.

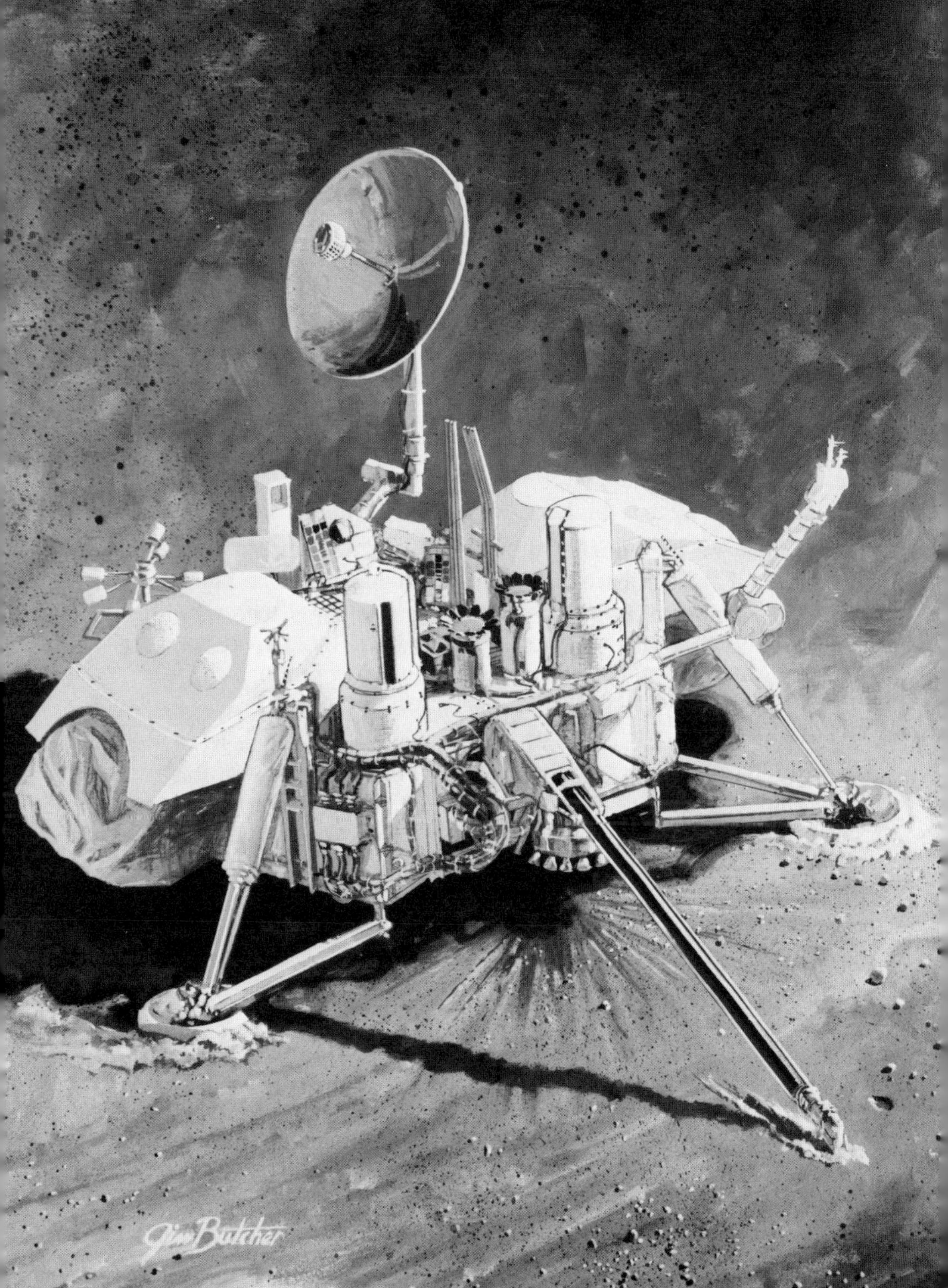
Jim Butcher

- Class III—life forms unknown on earth. They can live in high temperatures and require little water.

- Class IV—organisms that could survive very low temperatures and need very little water. Some scientists think that these organisms might be rock-eaters (Petrophages) that are able to extract water and nourishment from rocks. Or the organisms could be ice-eaters (Crystophages) that live off the permafrost—ice trapped under the ground.

The Viking lander's automated laboratory tested the Martian soil for the existence of a variety of living creatures, active or in frozen hibernation. Three suppositions were made, around which experiments were conducted, each one designed to detect a certain biological activity:

First: If there are any living organisms in Martian soil, perhaps they extract carbon from the atmosphere and use it to build a mixture of elements, compounds, like plants do on Earth. A small sample of Martian soil scooped up by the "surface sampler arm" of the Viking lander. The sample is dropped into the laboratory and the soil is tested chemically and electronically to determine if any living organisms have built compounds to produce food.

Second: Food may be eaten. This experiment is very simple. A sample of Martian soil is placed into a small chamber in the laboratory. Then a few drops of liquid food are placed in the soil. After a while very sensitive instruments are used to measure whether or not organisms have eaten the food.

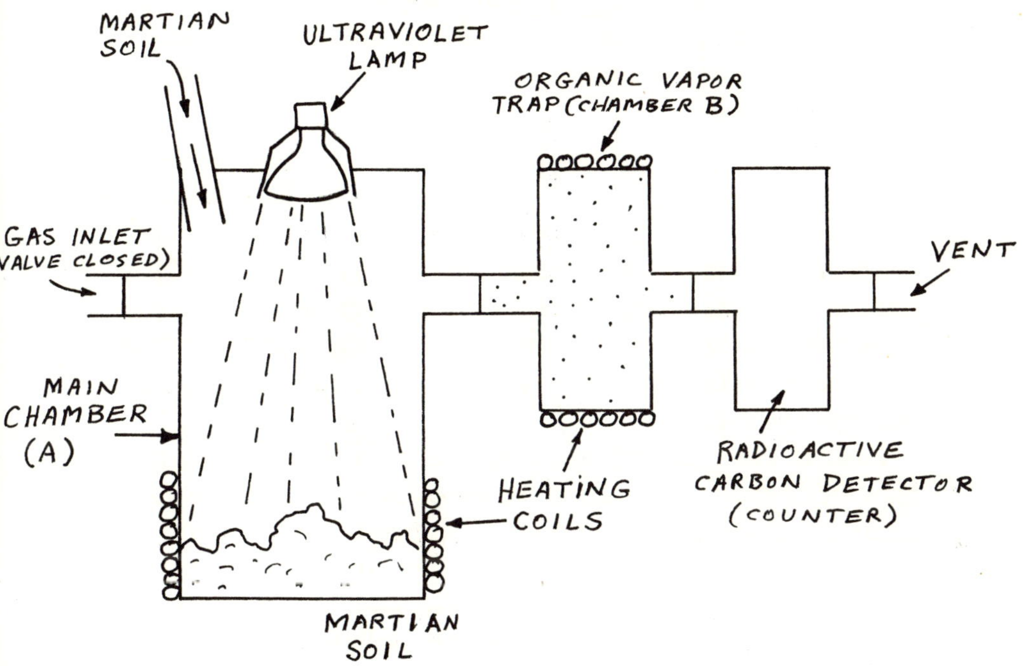

Viking soil sample test to determine if there are Martian organisms manufacturing food.

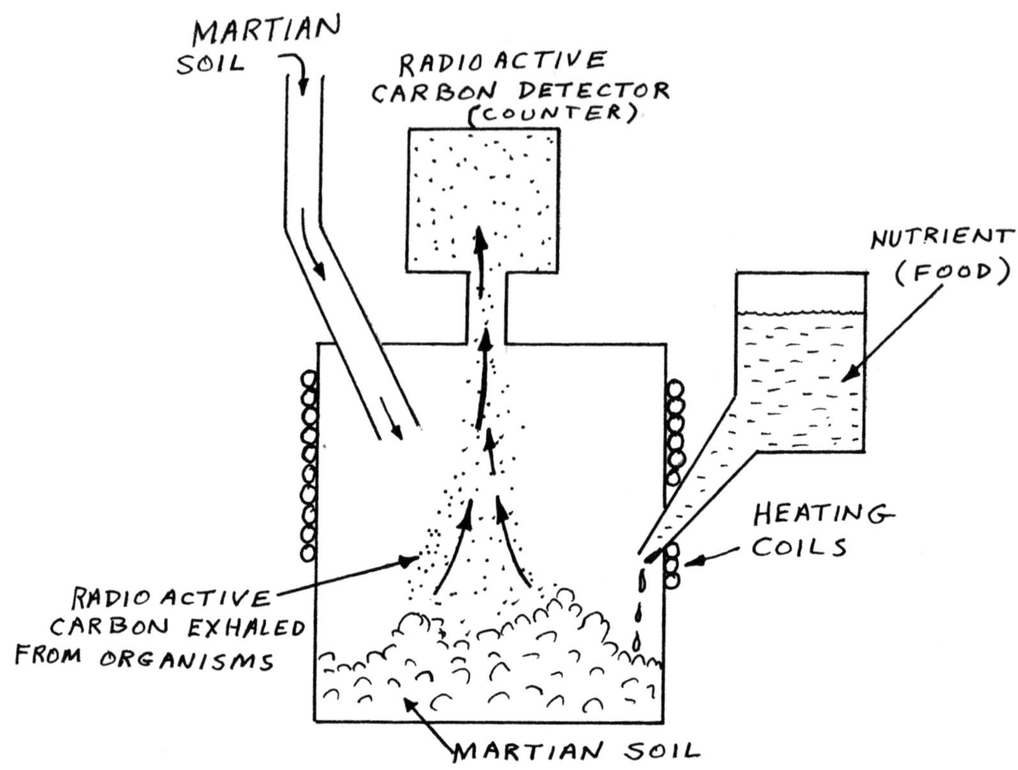

Viking experiment to determine if food is being eaten by Martian organisms.

Third: The air in the lab may be affected. This experiment simply measures the various levels of gases in a small chamber. Called the Gas Exchange Experiment (GEX), this test can determine whether or not organisms are breathing the atmosphere in the chamber.

Scientists are still arguing over the results of these experiments, but right now there is no strong evidence that any form of life exists on Mars. In the future, NASA may send a roving mini-laboratory to Mars so that many different locations on the planet can be tested for the existence of life.

Suppose we were to make contact with another civilization, what then?

How would aliens react to the idea of a civilization of human beings? By contacting other worlds, are we threatening our own? A hundred questions come to mind concerning other civilizations. Are they far advanced? Are they peaceful or warlike? What should we tell others about ourselves? Would we be able to understand alien languages? Are other civilizations capable of reaching our planet? Can we defend ourselves against an invasion of starships?

What would happen if we made contact with a more advanced civilization than our own? We might be lucky enough to receive a great deal of knowledge about the universe, knowledge that we might otherwise not have acquired for centuries, including maps of the galaxy, advanced observations, and explanations of the physical universe. We might learn about other cultures and how they solved social, physiological, and political problems. We might even learn the secret of survival as a planetary society.

On the other hand, perhaps aliens might consider Earthlings no more than a subculture to be enslaved for their own ends. Or, worse, we might be considered a much lower form of life, such

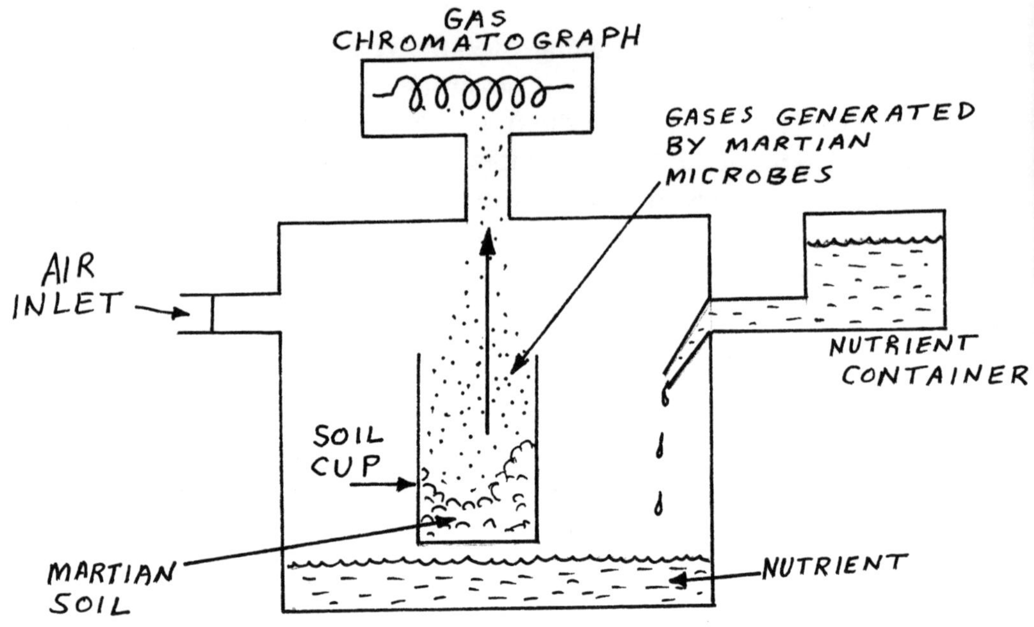

Viking test to measure change in atmospheric gases if an organism is breathing in the chamber.

as cattle or other animals, and barely be tolerated. An alien society might even decide to exterminate the planet of its "microbe life." Or perhaps the aliens have had terrible experiences with other societies, therefore they take immediate battle action to strike a mortal blow before asking questions.

We probably are not yet ready for contact with other civilizations. We need to develop first as a society at peace with itself in order to deal with other worlds.

One day, we will be ready to venture out into the far reaches of space. We will leave our familiar solar system far behind and become space pioneers. We will ride aboard spacecraft so advanced in their design that we cannot even imagine them at this time.

Chapter 6

The Future—The First Voyage

The time has come. Years of technological and sociological development have brought us the scientific breakthroughs we need to make the great journey to the stars. New fuels, new engines, advanced electronics, fantastic life support systems are all a reality now. Space colonies and huge orbiting laboratories and electric power stations have been in operation for decades. Colonies have been established on the moon and Mars, and remote research installations have been built on the moons of Jupiter and Saturn. We have even landed roving mini-labs on the surface of Pluto. The time is right, and we are about to begin our life-long journey to the stars.

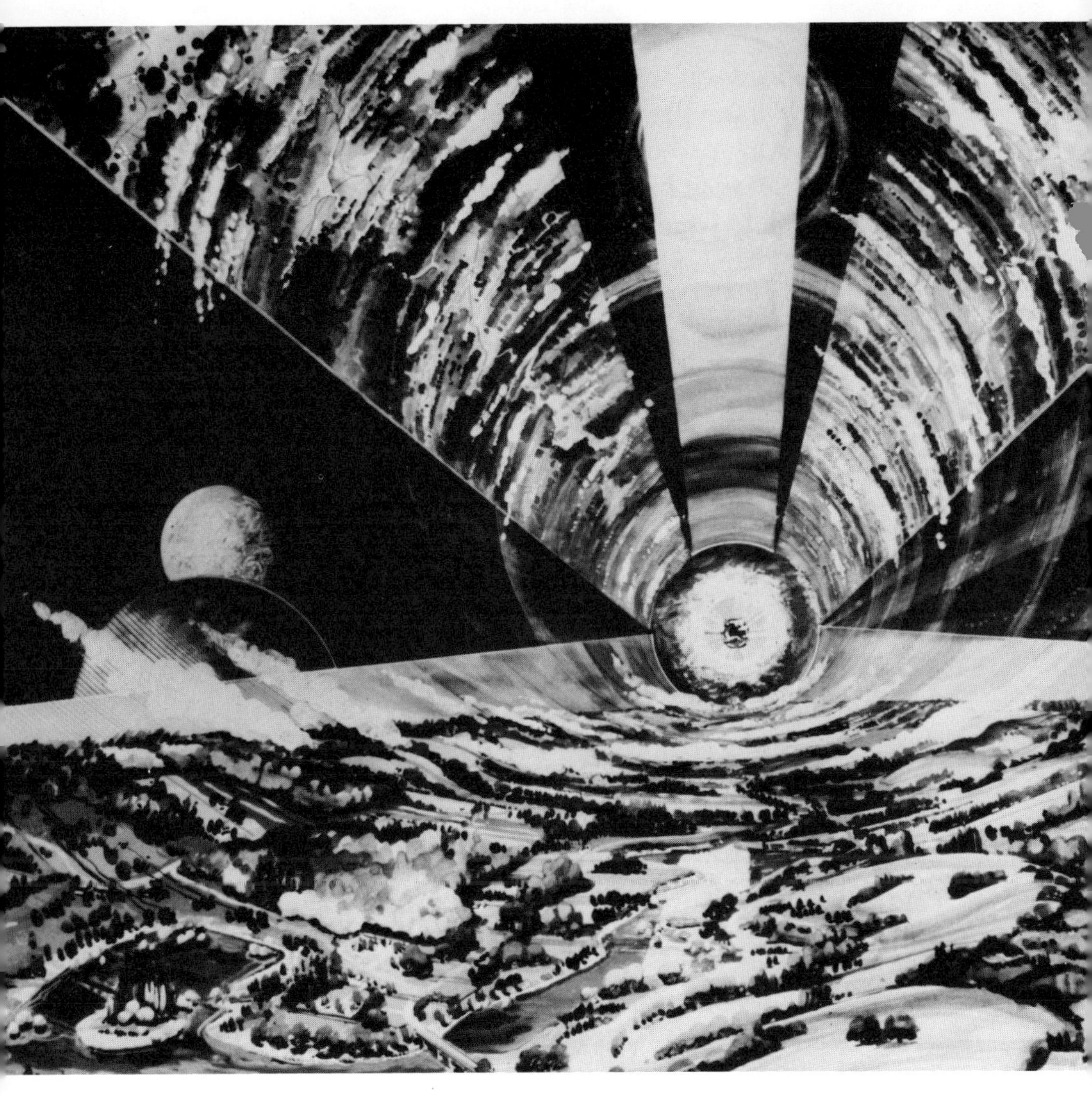

Artist's conception of space colony.

Let us think about the enormous distance we are attempting to span. We face the challenge of making a 26-trillion-mile journey to Alpha Centauri, or a 36-trillion-mile trip to Barnard's star. Suppose our spacecraft could travel at 10 percent of the speed of light—that is, 18,600 miles per second, or almost 67 million miles per hour. Even at this fantastic speed, it would take more than 43 years to make a one-way trip to the nearest star, Alpha Centauri. And it would be extremely difficult to construct a spacecraft to travel at even 1 percent of the speed of light in the next 100 years. But even if we did, a one-way trip to Alpha Centauri would last more than 430 years. So you can see that the problem is that we cannot travel fast enough to make a short-duration trip to a star, and we cannot live long enough to complete a long-duration journey.

Aside from the challenges of speed and time, there are the problems of carrying tremendous amounts of fuel and supplies needed to last for many decades.

What kind of rocket engine could possibly endure such a long trip? Perhaps the answer lies in atomic energy.

Some scientists feel that a special type of fusion-process engine called "deuterium, deuterium fusion" can accelerate a spacecraft to 10 percent of the speed of light or 67,000,000 miles per hour. It may be possible to use some very advanced form of atomic power to reach the stars. One scientific concept is called an "interstellar ramjet." Here is how it would work:

The space between the stars is not really empty. There are atoms floating around—not many, but they are there. There are from 1 to 1,000 atoms for each cubic centimeter (cc) of space. Most of these are hydrogen atoms. And hydrogen happens to be a good fuel for an atomic fusion rocket. So scientists think that an interstellar ramjet engine can be designed to use these hydrogen atoms for its operation.

Basically, such a spacecraft would consist of a giant scoop, shaped like the mouth of a trumpet and 75 miles in diameter. The scoop would also be a super-conducting magnet to gather up hydrogen atoms. Rockets would accelerate the spacecraft to the ramjet operating speed—that is, the speed at which the magnetic scoop can collect enough hydrogen atoms to keep its fusion engine going. Once it is at operating speed, the regular rocket engines are shut down and the interstellar fusion engine takes over. Since the spacecraft gathers its fuel along the way, there is no limit to the distance it can travel. This type of atomic rocket may be capable of accelerating a craft to 20 percent of the speed of light. Of course, the design, development, and operation of such an advanced craft may be several hundred years off.

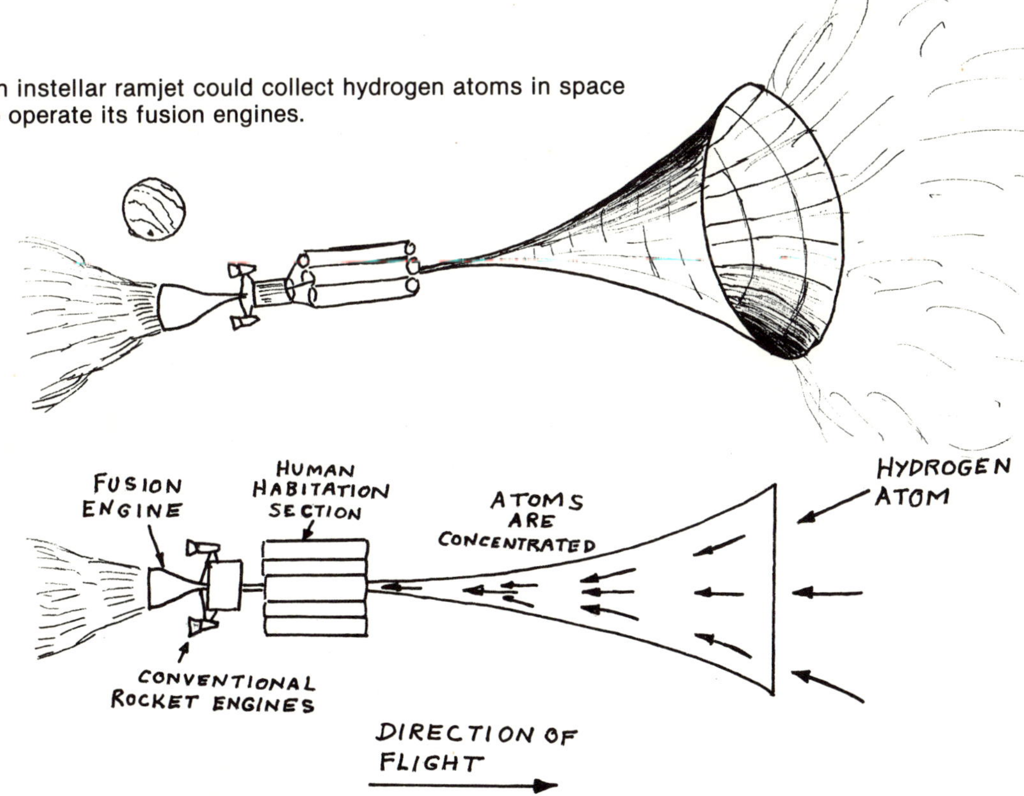

An instellar ramjet could collect hydrogen atoms in space to operate its fusion engines.

Then there is the Orion Nuclear Pulse Jet Interstellar Ark. This far-out spacecraft would ride the shock wave of a nuclear explosion. The spacecraft ejects a series of small hydrogen bombs which explode behind the craft. The shock wave from the explosion strikes the surface of a "pusher plate," thereby propelling the spacecraft. A huge shock absorber assembly prevents the living section of the craft from being jolted by the explosion. Such a spacecraft would carry about 300,000 hydrogen bombs and eject them at a rate of 1 per second. After 10 days of acceleration, the spacecraft would be traveling about 22 million miles per hour (one-thirtieth the speed of light). At this speed, a round trip to Alpha Centauri would take about 260 years (not including a stopover).

In approaching the problem of traveling to the distant stars, scientists usually assume that such a journey can last 100 years or more, longer than the span of human life. Perhaps, say scientists, one of the answers may be to place people into a state of suspended animation. In other words, suppose the crew of a spacecraft were to be put into "deep freeze," a state that is experienced by certain low-level life on Earth. The rocket could be traveling for 50, 100, or 200 years, while the passengers were "asleep." Near the end of the journey a computer would slowly bring the people out of their deep freeze and, in effect, wake them up. In this way a 200-year journey might appear to be merely a few months of traveling.

But that is a pretty drastic step to take. There might not be many people who would be willing to be frozen and hope that a computer would operate for 200 years to awaken them at the end of the trip. However, scientists do have other ideas about traveling to the stars.

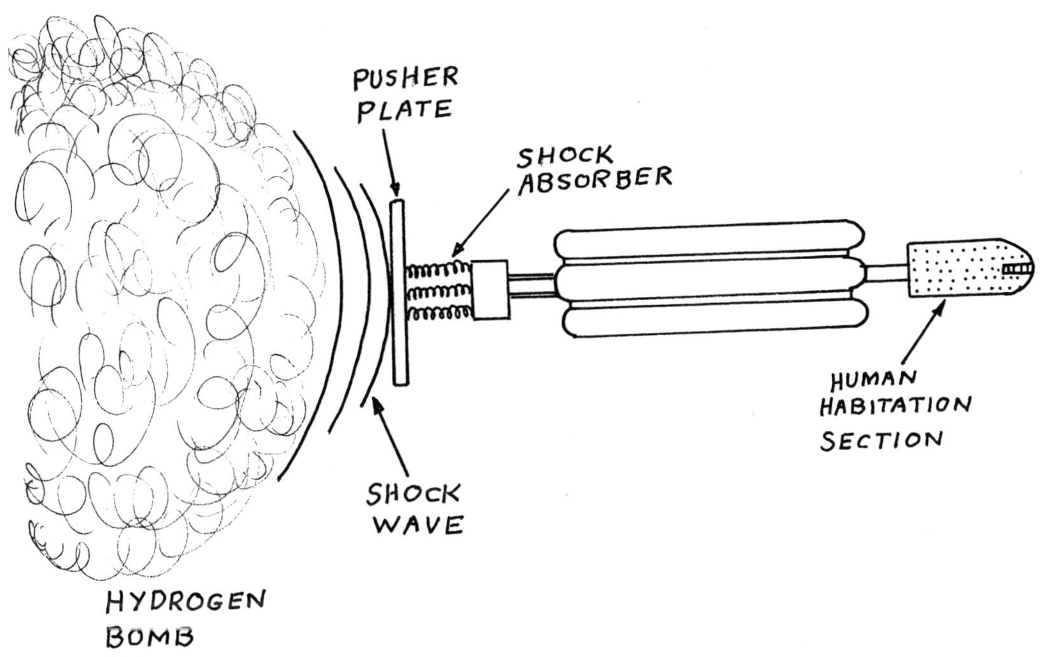

The Orion Nuclear Jet Interstellar Ark is designed to be propelled by a series of atomic explosions.

It is possible to change time itself.

According to Einstein's theory of relativity, it is impossible for anyone to travel exactly at the speed of light. But it is possible to travel at speeds very close to that of light. And as one begins to approach the speed of light, strange things happen. For one thing, time as we know it, is not the same.

Einstein's theory is that time slows down as one approaches the speed of light. So if you were traveling at 99 percent of the speed of light, you would age much more slowly. Let us say that your spacecraft is heading for Barnard's star at almost the speed of light. According to Earth time, it would take the spacecraft 12 years to make a round trip. But, upon your return to Earth, you would have aged only 2 years. This effect is called "time dilation." If a spacecraft could travel at nearly the speed of light (say 99.99 percent), it would be able to reach the center of our galaxy, over 30,000 light-years away, in an amazing 21 years as measured by the ship's clock. And even more astounding, a journey of only 28 years, ship's time, would bring you to another galaxy more than 100,000 light-years away.

Or we might get to the stars by traveling for hundreds of years, living and dying aboard a spacecraft which acts as a substitute home planet for many generations of people. Assembled in orbit around the Earth is an enormously large vehicle powered by fusion engines using deuterium (also called heavy water, H_3O). Special giant tanks capable of storing the fuel for hundreds of years carry some 300 million gallons of this water-like liquid. Located at the aft section of the craft is a fusion electrical power plant which will supply the community and the spacecraft with its energy. There are also energy storage systems

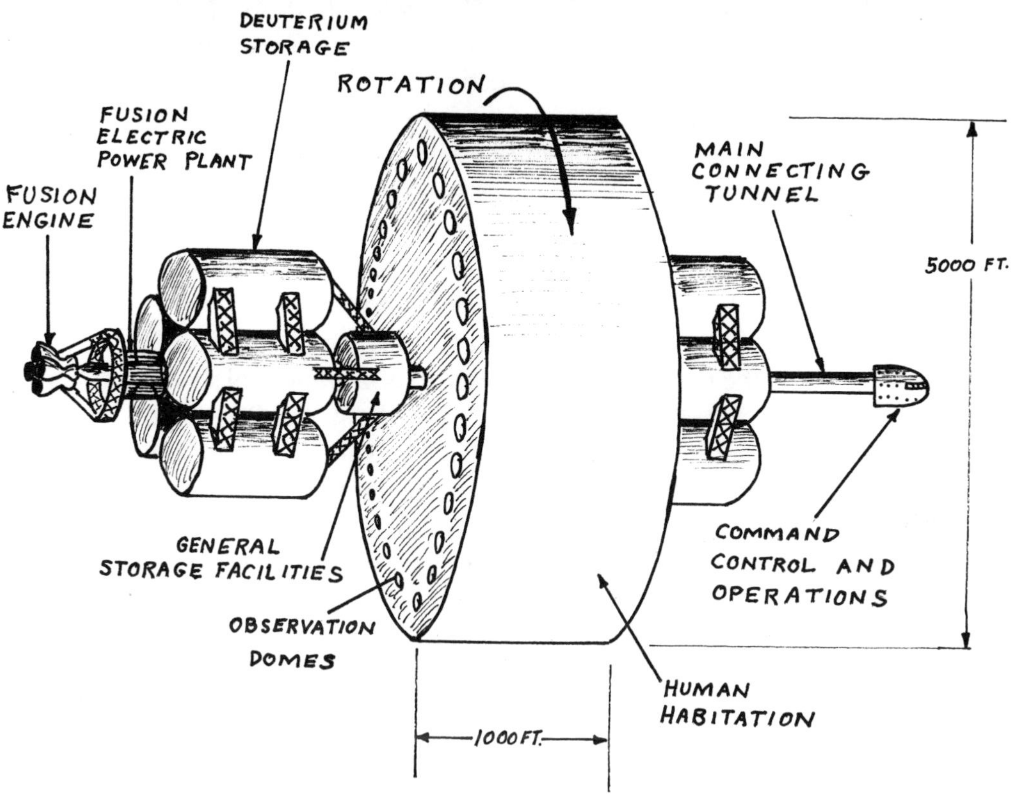

Design for an interstellar spacecraft.

to supply energy while emergency repairs are made on the main power plant. There are also a number of back-up power plants.

The command control and operations section are located at the front end of the craft. This section contains the electronic controls, computers, navigation, communications, and other systems. The quarters for on-duty personnel, along with crew dining and recreation areas, are also located here. Navigators monitor the ship's course and attitude, engineers watch the engine performance and power plant operations, electronics specialists maintain the control and other systems.

The most impressive part of the starship is the human habitation section—the main living area—which is a cylindrical section measuring 2,000 feet long and 5,000 feet in diameter. On each of its flat sides, there is a series of large observation domes. This huge habitation section rotates fast enough to develop a 1G force—that is, gravity equal to that on Earth. The human community section contains all the life support accommodations required for a natural lifestyle. There are homes, shopping centers, recreation areas, schools, houses of worship, food-growing areas, manufacturing facilities—nearly everything one would find back on Earth.

Now at last we are off on our voyage to the stars. We glance down at the soft green and blue glow of the cloud-adorned Earth. The excitement within us rises to fever pitch as the spacecraft commander gives the order to turn on the main bank of fusion engines. For a long time there seems to be no noticeable motion of the huge vehicle. But eventually we become aware that the Earth is slowly receding. Our craft has exceeded 25,000 miles per hour, and we are leaving Earth's orbit. Within hours the disc of our home planet has shrunk to the point where we can no longer distinguish the shapes of continents. We are traveling at 100,000 miles per hour; two hours later the craft is piercing the blackness of space at 300,000 miles per hour. Behind us the Earth is a tiny bright disc of light and ahead shines a bright light with a slightly reddish tint—the planet Mars.

In a few days we thrill at the sight of the red planet a mere 50,000 miles to our left. As we pass, we receive a message of congratulations and good wishes from the citizens of Mars. And still our spacecraft continues to increase speed. A week later we have reached 5,000,000 miles per hour and are approaching the giant of our solar system—Jupiter. Each time the spacecraft passes a planet, there is a surge of excitement and joy. For even at these far distances the sight of a planet reminds us that we are still within our home solar system. Another week passes; we are racing along at 10 and finally 15,000,000 miles per hour. We pass Saturn with its beautiful rings, then Uranus, then Neptune. The ship has been traveling for several months and is beginning to attain very high speeds. You watch our sun become smaller and smaller until it looks like any of the other yellow lights in the sky. Our destination star also appears as an ordinary yellow light.

Finally one day (the day and night cycles are maintained on

Photograph of Jupiter and its cloud system taken from Pioneer 10, 1½ million miles away. Jupiter's Red Spot is on right, shadow of moon Io on left.

the spacecraft), you are told that we are passing the small, cold and dark world of Pluto, the planet on the outer edge of our solar system. You rush to the observation rooms and peer out into the everlasting night. We cannot see the tiny globe that marks the end of our corner of the galaxy, but we all know that we have made the final exit. We are now in the realm of infinity and have become a wandering tribe, braving the vast sea of space in a lifelong voyage of exploration. With a full commitment to the future and complete faith in our destiny, we have become true citizens of the universe.

Suppose that your ship were to approach the speed of light. You look back at the earth's sun and notice something different. Its color has changed. It is no longer yellow, but more a yellowish-orange. Then you look at the destination star. It has turned a yellowish-green. The ship's commander explains that because of the spacecraft's extremely high speed, you experience a strange phenomenon called the Doppler effect. The Doppler effect causes stars to apparently change colors as the spacecraft goes faster and faster. The light from the destination star, since we are moving toward it, is turning blue. This is called a "blue shift." The star we are leaving is turning red. This is called a "red shift."

As the craft picks up speed, the sun or star that we have left behind is now an orange color, and the destination star is green. The Doppler effect is becoming more noticeable. Later we see that the home star behind us is now a bright red, and the destination star is a crisp blue. But to our amazement, all the stars in the direction in which we are heading are also beginning to change color. The closer ring of stars around the destination star is green. The outer ring is greenish yellow, and the stars farther away are the normal yellow.

The stars behind us are changing to orange and yellow-orange. You stare in wonder as the craft goes even faster. Suddenly something unbelievable happens. The home star, which was deep red a little while ago, has disappeared—it's no longer there. You turn quickly and look toward the front of the spacecraft. The destination star has also disappeared. The spacecraft commander has a simple explanation. The red and blue shifts of the stars are so extreme that the light, which is a form of energy, is no longer the type of light that can be seen by human eyes. The light from the home star is now infrared energy, which is invisible to the eye. The light from the destination star is ultraviolet energy, also invisible to the eye. That is why both stars disappeared. If the spacecraft slowed down, both stars would become visible again. But the spacecraft is speeding up.

Where once the home star had been, there is now a black disc —pitch-black, without any stars. The same sight appears ahead, a black disc where there was once the destination star. Also, a great portion of the universe around the home star and destination star is a rainbow of colors: bands of red, orange, and yellow, behind; violet, blue, green, and yellow ahead. Only a band of stars around the side of the spacecraft remains yellow.

As the spacecraft continues to accelerate, the black discs behind and ahead grow in size, as though they were consuming the entire universe. It seems like a giant hand is putting out the flickering stars. For a long time you watch the infinite dome of stars first burst into a rainbow of color and then disappear. A sense of terror grips you, for the discs of blackness have now all but devoured the universe. A few bands of crimson and violet stars flicker and fade. What is left is utter blackness, except for a single ring of bright yellow stars circling the speeding rocket.

If your spaceship does not travel at speeds close to that of light, it is designed to be home to many generations of space voyagers. Your children and your children's children will never set foot on land. Only your descendants will ever have a chance to settle once more on the surface of a planet because the starship will travel through interstellar space for nearly 400 years.

The children of the starship will know only the confines of their small world. They will never know the pleasure of sailing across an ocean, or standing in a large, grassy field with the wind blowing briskly. Parents will tell children about the Earth. There will be films and machines that simulate parts of the Earth to familiarize new generations with life on a planet. Computers will store all the knowledge needed to survive in a new world. Generations will come and go as the starcraft drifts across the void. Ultimately, the great-great-grandchildren of the first voyagers to leave Earth, 10 generations in the future, will arrive at their new home in the universe. They will tell many stories about their ancestors, the first pioneers who left a small planet trillions of miles away to search for other worlds.

Index